SECOND EDITION

THE 5 FOUNDATIONS OF THE
MODERN WORLD

A Student's Guide to World History

Volume 2

The Columbian
Exchange

Globalization and
Acceleration

The Rise of
the West

Industrialization and
Capitalism

Nationalism and
Democracy

Curtis F. Morgan

Kendall Hunt
publishing company

Cover image © Shutterstock.com

Kendall Hunt
publishing company

www.kendallhunt.com
Send all inquiries to:
4050 Westmark Drive
Dubuque, IA 52004-1840

Published in the United States of America

TABLE OF CONTENTS

ACKNOWLEDGMENTS

The author wishes to thank the students, faculty, staff, and administration of Lord Fairfax Community College for their moral support during the production of these two volumes. In particular, the constructive criticism of Dr. Jim Brumbaugh, Professor of Economics, and Anna Gruber Kiefer, Adjunct Professor of History, materially improved Chapters 4 and 5 of this work. The comments on *Volume 1* from my HIS 111 (World Civilizations to 1500) students were also influential on the approach to and writing of this second volume.

PROLOGUE

A GUIDE FOR THE PERPLEXED

The study of mankind's history is the most important study there is. As an individual person, you consult your "history" (your memories of your past) every day, even perhaps every moment. "History" is quite simply the record of what humanity recalls about *its* past. It influences every other human endeavor, scientific or creative. To make or discover something "new," you first have to know what is "old" (established). History may seem complicated (and it is), but really there are just three things to keep in mind about it:

First of all, History is, of course, concerned with *time,* specifically with that stretch of time we call the *past.* Already we run into a limit. We cannot know the future (fortunately, perhaps), so our knowledge is limited to the present and the past; and even our knowledge and understanding of those are imperfect. But we can start there: History concerns itself with human actions in the *past* and how those actions affect our *present.* We mark points in time by using **"dates."**

The second factor in History is *space.* This encompasses the physical environment around all of us, living and dead, specifically those portions of the planet's surface capable of supporting human existence; the oceans, the Himalaya mountain peaks, Antarctica (to name just three) have never sustained human habitation. However, within this limitation (environments capable of sustaining human habitation), there is surprising diversity. One of the things that make History interesting is looking at how different human groups have adapted to the Earth's diversity. To study History is to study humans, and to study humans one must study the whole world:—its unity *and* its diversity. And each place has affected all others. No human community has lived completely in a "vacuum." It used to be customary for Americans to be taught that their nation evolved in a new, isolated "virgin" continent, with minimal outside influence. But that view is discredited today. The United States has always existed in an inhabited and complicated world, and (willingly or unwillingly) interacted with it. And so has every other human community. You could call this the realm of "**places**."

So humans have existed in specific *times* and *spaces*. Together (and separately), these are difficult for our minds to take in.

But there is a third dimension, which I somewhat loosely call *life*. By this I mean existence itself. When I think of "human life" or "human existence," I think of it on two levels or planes: "macro-humanity," the totality of humans wherever and whenever they lived; and "micro-humanity," the unique lives of individual humans. A few (a *very* few) were known to many others and are the subjects of traditional history and biography. However, the vast majority of humans who have ever lived were known by only a very, very few (their immediately family members, their communities, possibly their immediate descendants who remember them). History concerns itself with this spectrum as well: the totality of humanity (in the form of its communities, political, economic, social, religious, cultural) and the beliefs, concerns and actions of (some few) individuals remembered for doing something important. Often we refer to these existences by recalling their "**names**."

Dates, places, names . . . they are the raw material, the granular *stuff* that makes up "history." And what makes studying history so mind-numbing. Perhaps you have suffered under the burden of forced memorization of lists of places, names, dates. Not only does it seem endless; it also seems so meaningless. What's the point?

Well, if collecting facts were all that History is, it *would* be pointless, like collecting a room full of bottle caps. Very interesting and enjoyable to someone, but *to what end?* Unless there is a *purpose* to studying History, it becomes both "pointless" and "endless."

But History's **purpose** is really, really simple: to try to recall humanity's story (by getting the facts right), in order to learn from it. All of humanity can, in this way, be studied like a single human's

Ball00025/Shutterstock.com

life. There is birth, childhood, young adulthood, and maturity. There are episodes of triumph, tragedy, success, failure, creativity, destruction . . . all influenced by what went before, all influencing what lies ahead. To be ignorant of one's history, the science-fiction author Michael Crichton once wrote, is to be a "temporal provincial . . . a leaf that doesn't know it's part of a tree." But to study History, one does more than collect facts (names, places, and dates); they must be sorted into a *pattern* that makes sense, like a jigsaw puzzle (or an Impressionist painting).

> *"To become a history, facts have to be put together into a pattern that is understandable and credible; and when that has been achieved, the resulting portrait of the past may become useful as well – a font of practical wisdom upon which people may draw when making decisions and taking actions."*
>
> — William H. McNeill, *Mythistory and Other Essays 1986*

History is endlessly fascinating once you realize that all the times, places, events, trends and *lives* have impacted *your individual life*, whether you are aware of it or not. The conditions of your existence (your health, wealth, attitudes, assumptions and power or powerlessness) are predetermined. If your life can be compared to a card game, would it not help you to know what the cards mean, how many cards are in the deck of which type, and some idea of the rules of the game?

> *"Whoever we are, the hopes, the triumphs, and the failures too of any human beings are properly of concern to us; in the moral economy of mankind they are also our own hopes and failures. In studying and sharing in them we know ourselves better, understand better who we truly have been and are, we human beings."*
>
> — Marshall Hodgson, *The Venture of Islam*

The purpose of this book is to present one way of interpreting the totality of recent human history by employing five ideas or categories to sort out all the dates, places, and names you will encounter along the way (like learning that a deck of cards has four "suits": hearts, clubs, diamonds, and spades). I developed these concepts when I began teaching World History in 2000. They operate as a framework, as a way to organize the facts of history, to develop patterns you can work from. I cannot claim authorship of the concepts themselves (I did not write the "script"), but I did select the concepts and determined how they are presented (I chose the "cast" and directed the "play"). Briefly presented, here are my **Five Foundations of the Modern World:**

1. **The Columbian Exchange:** The biological and ecological consequences of the discovery of the Americas by Europeans. More than any other factor, this process (still continuing) made possible . . .

2. **The Rise of the West:** The process of increasing global political, economic, and cultural dominance by Europe and its colonies in the Americas, Australia, and South Africa ("neo-Europes"). This process was both aided by *and* accelerated the spread of the next three Foundations.

3. **Nationalism & Democracy:** The radical shift in human governance models produced in Europe and spread around the world, freeing some while enslaving others, that grew from two linked ideas: **(a)** that the individual's highest loyalty is to an organized, self-governing "nation-state," *and* **(b)** that government's law-making and enforcement functions ("right to rule") are granted by the citizens, not by a superior hereditary or religious authority.

4. **Industrialization & Capitalism:** Beginning around 1800, the way human beings produced everything they needed to make material life possible, pleasant, and convenient changed drastically. Formerly, everything needed or wanted was made individually by hand; since 1800, mechanical devices ("machines") mass-produce all we need (even food!). This innovation (born in the "West") was made possible by *and* accelerated the transition to **capitalism,** an economic system that emphasizes **(a)** individual and corporate property rights, **(b)** a regulated free market

for exchange of goods and services, and **(c)** "wealth creation" using sophisticated credit and investment mechanisms (banks, stock exchanges, etc.).

5. **Globalization & Acceleration:** Finally, two more linked processes that were set in motion in ancient times, gradually intensified, and then exploded after 1492, when, for the first time, the *entire planet* (not just Eurasia) was brought into a single economic, political, and cultural "world system." This process has only continued to accelerate in your lifetime. The devices you depend upon, and the worldwide information-technology complex *they* depend upon, are products of these processes, spurred by the discoveries of the 1490s and deeply influenced by the new ideas and technologies developed by the West.

These are the colors on the palette of modern human history. Their **interaction** creates the unique pattern of human existence. As you begin your study of World History, I trust you will find this guide useful in putting names, places, and dates ("facts") together into a coherent framework. You will then be able to *understand* the totality of human history, and get a vision of your individual place in the story.

THINKING IN TIME

Write a paragraph essay about yourself, using as a framework the "three axes of existence" described above. Specifically, describe your place in

- *Time* (When were you born? How old are you?)
- *Space* (Where were you born? Where do you live now? What do you call "home"?)
- *Life* (What is your family like? How many generations have you personally touched? Who knows you? What roles do you play in life?)

Conclude with a reflection on the ways you are *connected* to other times, other places, and other people. You are a *leaf*; now describe your *tree*. (If you have done any genealogical research, feel free to briefly describe your findings.)

_____

_____

_____

_____

_____

_____

_____

_____

_____

_____

_____

_____

_____

_____

_____

_____

_____

_____

_____

_____

FOUNDATION 1

THE COLUMBIAN EXCHANGE

The Columbian
Exchange

Globalization and
Acceleration

The Rise of
the West

Industrialization and
Capitalism

Nationalism and
Democracy

Let the sky rain potatoes.

—Falstaff in Shakespeare,
The Merry Wives of Windsor, Act V, Scene 5

[As] for the natives, they are neere all dead of small Poxe,
so as the Lord hath cleared our title to what we possess.

—John Winthrop, governor of
Massachusetts Bay Colony, 1634

There are very few real "turning points" in World History; moments, actions or events that, if altered in some way, would result in massive changes "down the line." A popular motif of science fiction is "time travel," whereby someone somehow is able to travel back in time and "change" the future. This is entertaining, but misleading. Reality is not like that. If you have read the previous volume of this Student's Guide (*The Five Principles of Civilization*),[1] you would know that the course of history is like a mighty stream that cannot be "dammed," or "diked," or diverted from its course just by changing one life or one event. The course of history (especially World History, driven as it is by long-term trends and fundamental climatic conditions) unfolds slowly and majestically. At best, at certain points, under certain conditions, the course of history can (perhaps) be "bent" rather than "changed."

Fourteen Ninety-Two is one of the few exceptions to this "iron law of time." The European Discovery of America was probably inevitable (it would have happened anyway), but the *manner* in which it occurred, the *speed* with which it occurred, and the *enormity* of the changes it set in motion were unprecedented in world history. Nothing like this had ever happened before, and nothing like it could ever happen again (although it was repeated in later centuries, on a much smaller scale, for instance in Australia and New Zealand). You may have heard the often-repeated saying that "history repeats itself." Well, 1492 is unrepeated and unrepeatable, for reasons you will soon "discover."[2]

---

[1] Curtis F. Morgan, *The Five Principles of Civilization: A Student's Guide to World History.* (Kendall-Hunt, 2016).

[2] Some people like to put "discovery" in quotation marks, claiming that Columbus could not have discovered something that was already there. This is nitpicking. If I stumble upon a new bookshop in my town, I have "discovered" it, even though it was already there and others knew about it. The fact is *I* didn't know about it; it is a "discovery" for *me.*

Of course, 1492 is a date that a lot of people remember, if only because of that nursery rhyme:

In Fourteen Hundred and Ninety-Two
Columbus sailed the Ocean blue . . .

Simple Definition of discovery
  • : the act of finding or learning something for the first time : the act of discovering something
  • : something seen or learned for the first time : something discovered

From Merriam-Webster's Collegiate® Dictionary, 11th Edition ©2016 by Merriam-Webster, Inc. (www.Merriam-Webster.com)

And especially if you grew up in the United States, Columbus has an undeserved status as the "first American." But thanks to the writings of Alfred Crosby (among others) we now realize that there is so much more to it than a mere "discovery."[3] Columbus opened the door to a process that has never stopped to this day. The transformation of the Americas by contact with Europe and Africa; the transformation of Europe and Africa by contact with the Americas; and the transformation of the world by the expansion of European culture was made possible by this process (see Foundation Two: "**The Rise of the West**"). Fourteen Ninety-Two not only changed the entire world, but also "stepped on the gas" of historical change; ever since, the *pace* of change in every area of human life has steadily increased (a topic we will return to under Foundation Five: "**Globalization and Acceleration**"). But before we examine the many effects of the Columbian Exchange, we need to look at what it is.

In a nutshell, the Columbian Exchange involved the **greatest transfer of plant, animal, human and microbial species in history.** As I said above, while you can find in the historical record similar transfers both before and after 1492, nothing had ever taken place on the same scale or with the same effect before, nor would ever again. The Columbian Exchange has now

---

[3] Alfred W. Crosby, *The Columbian Exchange: Biological and Cultural Consequences of 1492.* (Greenwood Press, 1972); *Ecological Imperialism: The Biological Expansion of Europe, 900-1900.* (Cambridge, 2004).

spread all the way around the world, and therefore cannot happen again (at least, not until humans arrive at another planet or travelers from another world find us). Before 1492, one could still notice separate biological "pools" across the globe; that is no longer the case. **Plants, animals, plagues and people** are now distributed more or less evenly around the world. This is the first instance of **Globalization**.

We can now begin to "unpack" the Exchange and look at its separate parts. Keep in mind as we proceed: The changes I describe under separate categories happened *simultaneously* and constantly impacted and influenced each other.

PLANTS

Crops are the primary reason this process is called an "exchange"—because vital plant species were trans*planted* in *both directions* from the 1500s on. So, we need to look at which plant species went where and the effects this development had on Europeans, Africans, and Native American alike.

To Americas

As you probably know, the exploration of the Atlantic was attempted to find a way around the massive African super-continent to open long-distance trade with Asian civilizations via the Indian Ocean. (When you were younger, you probably heard about the obsession with "spices" but it was far more involved than that). The Portuguese first found the way around the "Cape of Good Hope" in 1488 and arrived at the west coast of India a decade later. The Spanish (Portugal's bitter trade rival) were faced with a dilemma: Should they use Portuguese-controlled routes to trade with Asia ("the Indies"), or find their own? Here is where Christopher Columbus (actually Cristoforo Colombo) comes in. He was the not the first to think of the western route to reach the east (nor, as we now know, even the first to *try* it; some Vikings spent a winter in Newfoundland in the 1060s) but he was the first to attempt to sail all the way to East Asia via the western route. This route (unlike the Indian Ocean one) was completely unknown and unexplored; *no one* known to 15th century travelers had ever crossed to India/China/Japan and returned to report it. Columbus didn't just "sail the ocean blue": He sailed off into the "Wild Blue." His sponsors (the King and Queen of recently united Spain) believed that he might not return. It was a gamble, but one they thought was worth making. If

Columbus failed, Spain lost three good ships and crews; if he somehow succeeded, the whole East–West trading "map" would be transformed.

Of course, no one knew there could be a massive continent blocking the way, —let alone two. Columbus's proposal was "debunked" by geographers who insisted that no European ship ever built could survive the sea voyage over thousands of miles of "open ocean" to arrive somewhere no European sailor had ever seen. And they were right. But Columbus went anyway.

Now, to make any sea voyage over such vast distances, the crew needed to eat for several weeks. This meant the ships had to pack food for the voyage. Therefore, they carried salted fish/meat along with "processed" bread (hard crackers/"hard tack"). This was a challenge: How long would the voyage to the "West" last? This influenced how much food you would need. The old story about sailors fearing to "sail off the edge" of the world is a myth; actually, they feared (with good reason) running out of food and water before they arrived anywhere. Sailing "east" they knew they could stop at African and Asian ports to get food and water; sailing west, "all bets were off." This was almost like flying to the moon. Whatever was needed had to be carried along.

"Almost." Because eating on the return trip would not be an issue. The explorers made sure to pack "seed corn," plant seeds to be used to grow and harvest food before the "packed lunch" ran out. In this way, several "absolute necessity" crops were introduced into the American environment for the first time. They took to the new soil with abandon, and became the dominant food crop species of the Americas, annihilating (with some human and animal assistance) native species along the way. Two staple grains deserve mention:

Wheat

Rice

Volosina/Shutterstock.com

pline_x/Shutterstock.com

It is no accident that wheat and rice were the first crops brought to America; they were probably the first food crops grown anywhere. The two together make up the bulk of staple crops grown in world history. Wheat is a "high and dry" plant that evolved in the semi-arid climatic conditions of the Middle East, and under human cultivation was adapted to the more temperate zones of the Mediterranean basin, Europe, and the northern tier of the Indian subcontinent (Indus and Ganges valleys). Rice, by contrast, is a "low and wet" plant that evolved in the semi-tropical river deltas of Southeast Asia, and soon spread throughout the lowland regions of East Asia to become the primary staple crop from the Ganges delta to northern Japan. It was also grown in parts of the Mediterranean coastal plain, which is why the Spanish were familiar with it. With seeds of both crops, the explorers of the Americas felt they had their "bases covered" for food production to tide them over for the return journey. It was soon discovered that the rice grew very well in the coastal/island areas, while wheat did well in the interior plains. As Europeans penetrated inland these two crops made permanent settlement possible, serving the same purpose they had in the "Old World."

Eventually, just about every crop known to Europeans was introduced into the Americas, displacing many plants and food crops grown by the natives. The most obvious and visual ecological transformation of the New World is found in the Mississippi Valley/Great Plains region of North America. Once home to broad prairies of open grassland ("steppe" in Asia), by the end of the 19th century, "amber waves of grain" dominated the landscape.

A third crop important to the "Columbian Exchange" had very different effects. This crop is strictly speaking not a "food" at all; in fact, it is poison in its pure form. However, beginning in the 16th century it became the single most "useful" crop in the world. Like olive oil in the ancient Mediterranean world, this substance was not consumed by itself, but as an additive that improved other

Hywit Dimyadi/Shutterstock.com

consumables. Today, nearly everything we eat (especially "processed" foods) contain surprising amounts of this chemical substance, now derived from other plants (particularly corn). I speak, of course, of *sugar*.

In terms of its historical and cultural effects, sugar is arguably the most important crop humans have ever grown. It was the first "cash crop" introduced to the Americas. A "cash crop" is one that is not grown for human consumption, but primarily for *sale*; its "end users" are usually not the people who produce it. It is often (in itself) not eaten or "consumed" but instead employed to produce some other product or substance, in this case a range of "secondary consumables" like molasses, rum, and powdered/crystal sugar for use in baking and (most profitably) as a sweetener for tea, coffee, and chocolate. (By the way, these beverages are another facet of the **Columbian Exchange**: Tea and coffee were first developed in Asia and Africa then brought to the Americas; chocolate was an American native introduced to the world.)

So far, we have looked at Eurasian food crops introduced *to* the Americas; the effects of this "invasion" will be examined later. But first, we must look at the other direction of the "Exchange": American crops that transformed the world.

From Americas

The Spanish came to the New World looking for gold; they found it, but in unexpected forms. As the *conquistadors* moved inland from the coasts of Central and South America, they encountered indigenous peoples, most of whom had been growing their own food for centuries. The Spanish were slow to adopt the native crops (and, for that matter, the natives didn't take to European crops either, even when forced to grow them). But, gradually, curiosity (and hunger) prevailed, and American crops were soon released into the wider world, where they continue to delight palates and transform cuisines. The best known of these are corn (properly, maize), chili peppers, tomatoes, and, most importantly, the potato. These "alien" plants were taken back to Europe and introduced into gardens and, eventually, farms. It was found that they all (especially the potato) adapted well to the varying soils and temperate climate, and succeeded brilliantly. In fact, the potato overcame initial resistance in Europe and China by its surprising adaptability. A plant that originated in the highlands of South America in rather dry conditions, the potato was found to thrive also in the *very opposite* ecology, the lowland, rain-lashed plains of Ireland, far north of its home.

The importance of these (and other) crops to the "Rise of the West" cannot be exaggerated. Poor, exhausted soils in Europe were brought back to life by these new food crops, and food production soared. So, in consequence, did Europe's population. In what I like to call a "feedback loop," increased food supply (made possible by American crops) led to increased population, which encouraged emigration of land-starved peasants to America; most of the newcomers were farmers, who brought yet more land under cultivation . . . But famously and tragically, this "feedback" could operate much less pleasantly. The potato was introduced to Ireland sometime in the 16th century (legend has it that wrecked ships from the Spanish Armada carried crates of potatoes) and flourished in the alien Irish/North Atlantic ecosystem. For over 200 years, the humble potato was the sole staple crop of the poor tenant farmers of Ireland.

rangizzz/Shutterstock.com

In the mid-1840s, a "blight" devastated the potato fields of Ireland, starving an estimated one million people. The English landlords and government largely turned a blind eye; as a result, thousands of desperate Irishmen (lured by the prospect of wage-paying factory jobs) fled to the United States. The lingering cultural effects are familiar every "St. Patrick's Day." I myself am descended from John Dougherty and Sarah McCormick, who arrived in Baltimore from Ireland in the 1850s.

The **key** here is what I like to call the *Feedback Effect*: New crops from the Americas (aided by European crops that flourished in the Americas) produced a *superabundance of food* that spurred a *population boom* in Europe and Africa. This in turn caused an *immigration spike* over the next two centuries. Many immigrants sought new lands on the western frontiers of the Americas; they produced *more* food . . . This process (with huge implications for the **Rise of the West**) continues as I write this: The United States is still the single largest food producer and exporter in the world, ably assisted by smaller countries such as Argentina. Another unfortunate side effect was the role American corn played in (1) fueling a West African population boom (thus increasing the available supply of slaves) and (2) supplying food for the slave ships bringing Africans to the Americas. Thus, crops discovered in America both freed millions of poor Europeans from poverty and oppression, *and* helped enslave millions of Africans. The final irony: The vast majority of African slaves were transported to the Caribbean and Atlantic coastal regions to grow **sugar**.

American food

Afro-Eurasian Immigrants

The Feedback Loop

ANIMALS

The second element of the "Columbian Exchange" (like the third) is much more a "one-way street." Until 1492, there were almost no domesticated animals anywhere in the Americas; the only exceptions were a species of turkey kept and bred by some Indian nations in North America, and the llama/alpaca employed in the Andes communities of South America. By contrast, Europe and Asia had been home to over a dozen species of animals that had been domesticated by humans for well over 10,000 years. Cattle, horses, sheep, pigs, oxen, chickens, goats, and water buffalo were familiar sights from the British Isles to Borneo. If you read Volume 1, *The Five Principles of Civilization,* you will know that these animals have helped make civilization itself possible in the "Old World." In addition, they provided milk and meat protein for the human diet, hide and hair for clothing, muscle power to pull plows and heavy loads (think of overland **Trade** here), and even organic fertilizer from their waste. When you consider the almost total lack of animals like these in the Americas before 1492, the achievement of sophisticated organized imperial societies by the Aztecs, Maya, and Inca is truly astonishing. But this lack also spelled their doom, as we will see.

The Horse

One of the most transformative creatures in human history is the *horse*. First domesticated on the Central Asian steppe thousands of years ago, it started as a "pony"-like animal not strong enough to bear the weight of a human, but capable of pulling a light load in a cart for short distances. Under selective breeding, the horse grew in size and power, and "split" into specialized breeds designed to pull heavier loads and plows, as well as wheeled "combat cars" (chariots). Eventually (sometime by the 9th century BCE), the backbone developed sufficiently to carry the weight of an armed man, and "cavalry" was born. The role of this one animal in the history of Word Civilization is immense. It not only assisted in agriculture, war, and trade, but also in animal husbandry, by greatly assisting in the herding of other animals (especially cattle). By the time of the discovery of the Americas, the Spanish had already established themselves as the world's premier breeders, trainers, and employers of horses. They had been herding cattle on horseback for centuries. They had driven the Moors from Spain on horseback. Therefore, it should be of no surprise that the Spaniards brought horses with them to the "New World." Not to do so was unthinkable.

Horses had roamed the plains of North America before the retreat of the glaciers after the last Ice Age. But they were much smaller (about the size of a Great Dane) than the horses we see today, and disappeared into extinction about 11,000 years ago. The (re)introduction of the horse into the Americas in the early 1500s was a major ecological event. Horses made possible the

mariait/Shutterstock.com

swift defeat of native armies during the initial conquest, and (as in Europe) greatly assisted the establishment of working farms and plantations, not to mention overland trade.

But a surprising twist in the story of the horse in America is the effect it had on the people already here in 1492. A number of horses escaped their Spanish masters and migrated to the Great Plains, reproducing at a phenomenal rate. Here, they were encountered by native hunter–gatherers who had subsisted (barely) for millennia, by hunting buffalo on foot. The horse was a revelation to these natives, who quickly captured and trained them. (A common Native American family name today is "Horsecapture.") They were soon using the height, speed, and maneuverability of the horse to peel off, isolate, and bring down buffalo. Bows and arrows made the work even easier. Because horses came into the plain of North America ahead of the Spanish armies, the "Indians" were able to take control of their primary food source and begin spending time creating a culture of their own. For about two centuries, the Sioux, Cheyenne, and other "First Nations" flourished exactly the way Huns and Mongols did in Central Asia, until they were systematically destroyed in the 19th century. This was in contrast to the Aztecs and Incas, who first encountered the horse as a weapon of "shock and awe" wielded by the *conquistadors*.

Stocksnapper/Shutterstock.com

Cattle

The primary reason the Spanish were so familiar with horses is that they had used them to control cattle for many centuries. The humble cow is one of the mainstays of the Western world. For thousands of years (since the dawn of Civilization itself) cattle have provided meat, milk, and hides for clothing and leather. Under human domestication, cattle are now one of the dominant species on the planet, so numerous that even their digestive gases are thought to contribute to global warming!

Canicula/Shutterstock.com

Taken to America, cattle began making gentle war on several plant species that could not tolerate being eaten, and slowly drove them into extinction, making room for varieties of grass that better tolerated animal mastication. Herded by horses and accompanied by sheep and goats that "cropped" the grass and brush at different heights, cattle transformed the Americas into the "meat locker" of the world.

Pigs

A final example of the "beastly battalion" that the Spanish introduced to the American continents is *Sus scrofa domesticus*, the pig or the hog that produces even more meat in proportion to its body size than the cow does. While pigs were "herded" (Pizarro, conqueror of the Inca, started life as a "swineherd"), they usually are content to follow their human masters around, feeding on whatever they can find. Their tendency to reproduce rapidly and take care of themselves with a minimum of human trouble even led the Spaniards to drop a few dozen on odd islands here and there, intending to return and slaughter a few later when needed. Spaniards would march for hundreds of miles, followed by another curly-tailed army trotting along behind. Many went "wild," which was fine for the Spanish, who knew they were easy to hunt, kill, and eat.

But domesticated animals also had a dark legacy, what Jared Diamond called the "Lethal Gift of Livestock."[4] The very same animals that made organized

---

[4] *Guns, Germs, and Streel: The Fates of Human Societies* (Norton, 1999), Chapter 11.

civilization itself possible by assisting the production of a permanent food sur-plus and fueling humanity's expansion are also responsible for more human deaths than all other causes, including war.

PLAGUES AND PEOPLES

This phrase is the title of William H. McNeill's classic study of the role of disease in human history.[5] The two parts are inseparable; the Columbian Exchange involved a massive shift in the demographics (population distribu-tion) of the planet, and disease played the single largest role in this change. It annihilated the native population; introduced African slave labor to the Americas and created the trans-Atlantic slave trade; and ushered in the **Rise of the West**.

The Lost Tribes

It is difficult to know just how many indigenous people were living in the Americas in 1492; the "Indians" themselves kept no written records at all; there were no censuses until the Spanish Catholic Church attempted to count them in the late 1500s; and it is hard to know how accurate that count was. A reasonable estimate is between 50 and 60 million Native Americans were

---

[5] He coins terms to describe the only two mass killers of human beings: microorganisms ("microparasites") and humans themselves ("macroparasites") which he discusses in another classic study, *The Pursuit of Power*. The use of "parasite" is apt, since in both cases, killing is a "side effect"; the point is to *exploit* (feed off of) the "host." Thus it can be said that war is a variety of "plague."

present in 1492; about a century later, the Church counted about 5 million in its care. If accurate, this means an approximate loss of 90% of the pre-1492 population, the most catastrophic loss of human life in world history.[6]

The primary cause of this disaster was not mistreatment by Spanish and Portuguese "*conquistadors*"; although there are numerous accounts of Spanish atrocities (most reported by the Spanish monk Las Casas), they could not begin to account for the swiftness of the depopulation of the Americas; many villages were wiped out that apparently never saw a Spaniard. The simple fact is that epidemic diseases (such as smallpox, typhus, malaria, bubonic plague, and measles, to name just a few) were suddenly released into the American continents and quickly attacked the natives, who had no acquired immunity to any of them. Any one of these biological scourges would have been devastating; *all* of them unleashed on an unprepared populace spelled a plague of unprecedented proportions.

How and why did this happen? We now know what the explorers did not: They were carriers of these diseases. But why were they not affected? Because they had acquired (through earlier exposure and survival) or inherited immunity to these diseases. Europe and Asia were the homes of these plagues, and Europeans had been repeatedly exposed to them for hundreds of years (going all the way back to the "Plague of Justinian" in the 500s). Those who were not able to cope died; those who managed to survive were able to reproduce and "pass on" their immunity to their children. But the germs themselves remained in the bloodstreams of the Europeans, and could easily "migrate" to infect the body of a person lacking the immunity. And how did the Europeans acquire this immunity? By constant exposure to the source of the germs: domesticated animals. Cows, pigs, sheep, and chickens fed and clothed Europeans and Asians, and made them sick. Native Americans lacked these animals, and therefore missed the "opportunity" of exposure and acquired immunity. The stage was set for a human tragedy of unimaginable proportions.

The long-term outcome of this disaster was the almost effortless re-populating of the Americas by Europeans seeking new lands and new opportunities,

---

[6] These figures are guesses at best. For a discussion of the various estimates (fraught with political and social controversy), see Charles C. Mann, *1491: New Revelations of the Americas Before Columbus* (Vintage, 2006), pp. 102–106.

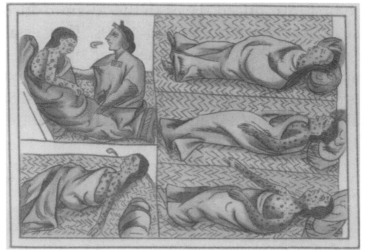

"Smallpox was introduced into Mexico by the Spanish expedition of Panfilo de Narvaez and raged through the Aztec capital Tenochtitlan in late 1520."

not least among these escape from political and religious oppression (see **Democracy**). Needless to say, Native Americans had their lands and opportunities taken away from them. However, they were not the only "losers" from the Columbian Exchange.

The Transplants

The mass die-off of Indians not only made room for Europeans. It also made possible the mass importation of slaves from West Africa into the New World. We see here not only the combination of "Plagues" and "Peoples" remaking the Americas, but also the key ingredient of "Plants": Columbus commented on the suitability of the Caribbean islands he visited for **sugar** planting, and the Spaniards attempted to use native labor to launch their sugar production operations. But the epidemics soon annihilated the local population. European "indentured" labor was tried, but these workers were "temporary" in more than one sense: Assuming they survived the heat and tropical diseases (most did not), they could leave service at the end of their "term" (often sooner). Sugar planters needed a labor force that was easier to control, better acclimated to the tropical/sub-tropical conditions, and more familiar with the sugar plant and sugar processing.

The Portuguese first introduced slaves to the Atlantic during their explorations of the west African coast in the mid-1400s. They established trading stations from the equator all the way to the Cape of Good Hope. Africans made available captured warriors and villagers from hostile tribes and bartered them for European goods, eventually including guns. So began one of the greatest humanitarian crimes in history, the Transatlantic Slave Trade.

joppo/Shutterstock.com

For almost 400 years (from the early 1500s to the 1880s—the leading slaving nation, Britain, outlawed the trade in the 1830s) Africans were taken across the ocean to work for European landowners seeking profits from production of "cash crops" like sugar, tobacco, and cotton. All of these products were useless in their "natural" state; but once "processed" into secondary products (molasses, table sugar, cigars, and cotton cloth) they could be sold at a huge profit due to their "added value." (See **Industrialization & Capitalism**) Unfortunately, African slaves were the cheap, often expendable labor necessary to the success of the system, so valuable that they became a major "commodity" themselves (hence the term "Slave Trade"), as their purchase price, low in Africa, meant a much higher sale price in America. This was because their unpaid *labor* vastly increased the value of the *land*, producing great wealth (*capital*) for the Europeans who were able to acquire a plantation in the New World. Slavery spread to every corner of the Americas, including (as we will see in the next chapter) silver mines.

The demographic consequences were immense; the cultural, economic, and eventually political effects even more so. The "African Diaspora" (Greek for "dispersion," "scattering," like seed) involved, over the span of some 300 years or so, and estimated 9.5 million people transported to the Americas, many of whom died on the "Middle Passage," many more in the horrendous working conditions of the sugar plantations. Yet many survived long enough to reproduce, managing to preserve and transmit a unique "African-American" culture that continues to influence and inspire art, music, and literature. The experience of slavery also fueled a fierce desire for freedom that motivated the "emancipation" movements of the 19th century as well as the "Civil Rights" movements of the 20th century (see **Democracy**). But there is a last "People" who owe their existence to the Columbian Exchange, one that combines all three demographic elements: "Afro-Euromericans."

The Hybrids

By the 17th century, intermarriage among European settlers, surviving indigenous Americans and some transplanted Africans produced a new people, known in our imperfect terminology as "Hispanics" (from the Spanish name for the first American island discovered, *Hispaniola*) or "Latin Americans" or "Latinos" (more obscurely; the "Latin" refers to the fact that Spanish and Portuguese are Latin-derived languages, unlike English, which is a Germanic tongue[7]).

Drawing on this mixed heritage, Latinos predominantly speak Spanish (with Portuguese in Brazil) and belong to the Roman Catholic Church (to which Spain and Portugal remained loyal during the era of the Protestant Reformation). They developed a unique cultural fusion of European, African, and Native American elements, most noticeable in music and dress. Stretching from the Rio Grande to the "Straits of Magellan," these people are the largest ethnic group ever to exist in the Americas, the living embodiment of the "Columbian Exchange."

---

[7] One might ask why French Canadian *Quebecois* are not also "Latin Americans": French is a Latin-based language too!

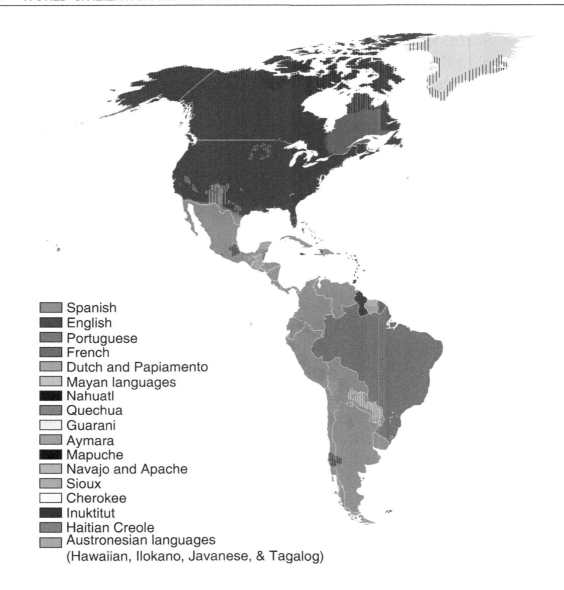

Spanish
English
Portuguese
French
Dutch and Papiamento
Mayan languages
Nahuatl
Quechua
Guarani
Aymara
Mapuche
Navajo and Apache
Sioux
Cherokee
Inuktitut
Haitian Creole
Austronesian languages
(Hawaiian, Ilokano, Javanese, & Tagalog)

CONCLUSION

The Columbian Exchange is the process that set "modern times" into motion, by opening the door to the four Foundations that follow: **The Rise of the West; Nationalism & Democracy; Industrialization & Capitalism; and Globalization & Acceleration.**

THINKING IN TIME

1. Make a bulleted list of the major elements of the Columbian Exchange, including *specific examples* of each.

_____

_____

_____

_____

_____

_____

_____

_____

_____

2. Believe it or not, *you* are a product of the Columbian Exchange; even if you are of Asian ancestry, your presence in North America is a testimony to the continuing pull of the Americas on the rest of the world. Think about your family and its heritage, and write a brief paragraph reflecting the role of the Columbian Exchange in your background. (If you worked on "Thinking in Time" from the Prologue, you may find those comments helpful. Elaborate on them.)

_____

_____

_____

_____

_____

_____

_____

_____

FOUNDATION 2

THE RISE OF THE WEST

The Columbian
Exchange

Globalization and
Acceleration

The Rise of
the West

Industrialization and
Capitalism

Nationalism and
Democracy

*"Why is it that you white people developed so much cargo
and brought it to New Guinea,
But we black people had little cargo of our own?"*

—"Yali" to Jared Diamond, 1972[1]

*Whatever happens we have got
The Maxim Gun, and they have not.*

—Hilaire Belloc[2]

The Rise of the West is the title of a classic book by William H. McNeill. It presents an interpretation of the entire human story by describing human civilization as a set of "primary" or "foundational" culture zones that grew up more or less under similar conditions, and that for most of history these civilizations formed a balanced "ecumene," or "World Civilization." Beginning about 1500 CE, this "balance" eroded, then collapsed, with one civilization (the "Far West," Europe) surging to planetary dominance politically, militarily, economically, and culturally. This "surge" is "**The Rise of the West.**"

Although Western Europe (or "Latin Christendom," to distinguish Western Europe from Greek Orthodox Eastern Europe) was already rapidly evolving in a unique direction before Columbus's ships dropped over the Atlantic horizon, the fact remains that the Discovery of the Americas, *more than any other event,* **accelerated** the expansion and development of Western Europe's civilization to global dominance by the 19th century CE. It must be kept in mind that Europeans *alone* (not Asians, Africans or

---

[1] Jared Diamond, *Guns, Germs, and Steel: The Fates of Human Societies* (New York: Norton, 1999), p. 14. "Yali's Question" was what drove Diamond to explore the roots of human inequality, and why Western societies are more materially wealthy and technologically advanced ("have more cargo") than non-Western societies. David Landes also addresses this topic in *The Wealth and Poverty of Nations.*

[2] Quoted in Ian Morris, *Why the West Rules—For Now* (New York: Picador, 2011), p. 12. The "Maxim" was an early machine gun, invented by an American, Hiram Maxim, during the Civil War. It appeared too late to influence that conflict, but greatly assisted the European imperial "Scramble for Africa" before the First World War. "They" are African tribesmen. Hilaire Belloc (1870–1953) was a French poet.

Muslim states) discovered the Americas, and therefore were able to explore and exploit the new continents with *no interference* from other civilizations or empires. It is therefore no accident that Western Europe recreated America "in its own image," converting it to what Alfred Crosby calls a "neo-Europe." (Others would soon follow: Australia, New Zealand, and South Africa; despite their geographical positions on the globe, they are in every sense "European.") **The Rise of the West** was made possible by **The Columbian Exchange.**

Before we move further, we need to familiarize ourselves with Europe as it was, before 1492.

The "Five Principles of Civilization"

In Volume 1 of *A Student's Guide to World History*,[3] I introduced the "Five Principles of Civilization," a way to understand the major influences of human history before 1492. These Principles are a great tool for quickly grasping Europe's "back story."

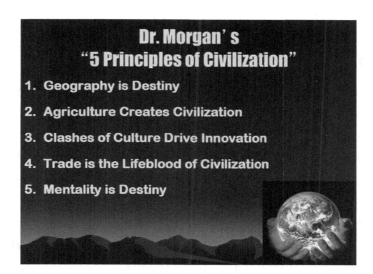

---

[3] Curtis Morgan, *The 5 Principles of Civilization: A Student's Guide to World History, Vol. 1* (Kendall-Hunt, 2016).

1. **Geography** (topography, climate, and resources) determines where and what crops can be grown, as well as influencing the operation of the other four Principles.
2. **Agriculture** provides a *food surplus* to feed cities, whose *specialists* (non-farming "professionals") create the complex social networks called **civilizations.** These soon find themselves in conflict with non-agricultural communities over scarce resources (water and arable land).
3. These **clashes of culture** spur technological **innovations** among the civilizations to control/expel the "barbarians" that surround them. ("Barbarians" also learn from "civilized" cultures, often becoming absorbed by them.)
4. Civilizations circulate *goods and ideas* among themselves and with "barbarians," this **trade** spurring yet more **innovation**, allowing civilizations to grow and develop like organisms.
5. Finally, this growth and development forms a civilization's unique **mentality** that shapes its own culture and its relations with other cultures (art, philosophy, religion, government style, trade/foreign policy and war-ways).

From Merriam-Webster's Collegiate® Dictionary, 11th Edition ©2016 by Merriam-Webster, Inc. (www.Merriam-Webster.com)

Asia's *Uniformity*

To fully understand why and how the West "rose," it helps to ask why the "East" did not. Some historians see this question as the one of the biggest in human history (Asia claims the majority of the world's population, after all) and have invented a term for it: the "Great Divergence."[4] They are struck by the affluence and technological sophistication of the East Asian civilizations (particularly China) and are puzzled as to why the **Industrial Revolution and Capitalism** did not develop there until the West imposed them on Asia in the 19th and 20th centuries.

One proposed explanation involves the role of **Geography.** By directly *comparing and contrasting* the physical forms of Europe and Asia, one can see ways that industrial innovation and economic growth were helped in Europe and hindered in Asia. It is noticed for instance that Asia largest geographical

---

[4] Kenneth Pomeranz, *The Great Divergence: China, Europe and the Making of the Modern World Economy* (Princeton, 2000); J-L Rosenthal and R. Bin Wong, *Before and Beyond Divergence: The Politics of Economic Change in China and Europe* (Harvard, 2011).

feature is the "Great Eurasian Steppe," an "ocean" of prairie grass stretching from Manchuria all the way to eastern Europe, running east–west along a broad belt north of the "**Agriculture** belt" where the major civilizations evolved (see map, center). By the time Columbus sailed, Asia was dominated by several enormous empires ruled by dynastic families descended from horse-nomads who conquered "civilized" Asia from the steppe; I call these regimes Asia's "steppe-children": The Ottomans in western Asia (the "Middle East"), the Safavids in Persia (Iran), the Mughals in India, and (after 1644) the Manchus in China (Qing Dynasty).

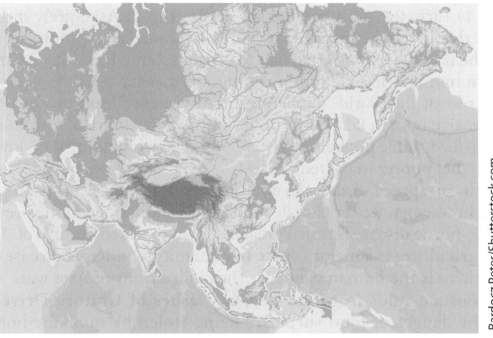

Bardocz Peter/Shutterstock.com

Despite appearances, all of these empires were effectively land-locked: look at the map again. All are hemmed in by massive mountain ranges and extensive deserts. Their coastal plains look out upon the Indian and Pacific Oceans, the largest open oceans on the planet; each leads "nowhere" and will not be crossed by sailing ships before Europeans do so in the 1500s. (Chinese "Star Fleets" explored the Indian Ocean in the early 1400s by not leaving sight of land; the same is true of Pacific navigation.) Thus, **Geography** affects **Trade** here: sea routes are limited and beset by "choke points" such as the Straits of Molucca. Most East–West trade will be *overland*, via the famous

"Silk Road" traveled by Marco Polo and a few others, but here **Clashes of Culture** come into play: the overland route goes either through or just alongside the Eurasian Steppe, meaning that nomadic herdsmen control these routes, opening or closing them at their whim. (This was a big reason why Columbus proposed sailing westward, to bypass this huge overland route.) So, **Trade (the Lifeblood of Civilization)** was constricted (you could say that Eurasia suffered from "hardening of the arteries.")

But there were more difficulties. **Agriculture Creates Civilization,** and Asia enjoyed bountiful harvests of wheat, rice, and other staple crops, but its farmers employed few domesticated animals. There were a couple of reasons for this: (1) Rice, the most productive staple crop in Asia, grew in flooded "paddies" that had to be managed by humans; animals were more harm than good to the fragile seedlings that had to be transplanted; and (2) Animals eat more than humans do. Asian population densities have always been higher than the rest of the world, demanding more intense food production *and* more intensive human labor to produce it. In short, animals cost more than humans to feed, while not being as useful in food production. The "downside" of this is a diet poorer in protein, as well as the use for human waste as fertilizer, which can spread disease. In addition, the fact that most Asian populations live in warmer, wetter climates close to the Equator, and the prevalence of parasite-borne disease is much greater. As was pointed out in Vol. 1 of this Guide, **Agriculture** is a major source of humanity's epidemic diseases.

Then there is the human element. The civilizations of Asia were vulnerable to constant raids from the steppe. **Clashes of Culture Drive Innovation:** the danger of food surpluses being stolen by nomadic horsemen drove the Asian cultures to invent systems of government demanding near-absolute control over society in order to organize some effective defense against them. The ultimate monument to this effort is the "Great Wall of China" that cost untold thousands of lives and unimaginable resources to build. And it had to be manned to be effective. So governments were almost as rapacious as the nomads were. Meanwhile, the major religions developed into ethical systems designed to "comfort the afflicted," that is, to teach Asians to accept their lot in life, hoping to "reincarnate" into a better one, or to withdraw (if possible) from the suffering of this life to eventually reach "Nirvana." This Asian **Mentality** created societies resistant to change or to an outlook whereby one could hope to improve one's lot in life through individual effort.

I present the previous paragraphs with a note of caution: Asia is an incredibly diverse place, full of a rich "crazy-quilt" of cultures and beliefs; but Asia's vast human family shared a set of circumstances and characteristics that set it apart from Europe, and **Geography** is the key. *All* of Asia's civilizations shared one circumstance in common: their *proximity to the steppe*. Europe was not as accessible from the steppe. And that has made all the difference.

Europe's *Uniqueness*

To understand what set Europe apart from the other civilizations stretching across the Asian supercontinent, we first need to *compare and contrast* the principal **geographical features** of each area. Europe is a *peninsula* extending westward from western Asia. Although extending from Asia, seemingly seamlessly, Europe is bounded on its eastern "frontier" by thick forests extending from Finland in the north almost to the northern shores of the

Kateryna Kon/Shutterstock.com

Black Sea. A narrow **steppe frontier** separated this forest from the Black Sea itself, which (together with the Caspian Sea and Caucuses mountain range) effectively "wall off" the European peninsula from Asia. (See map.)

While Asian civilizations were vulnerable to steppe attack all along a frontier stretching thousands of miles east–west, Europe was blessed: first, its *steppe frontier* was shorter (a few hundred miles or so) and oriented north–south. Also, unlike China, India, and Persia/Iran, Europe's heartlands were situated much further away from the Central Asian "base areas" of the steppe people. Thus, steppe nomad invasions (the Huns in the 400s CE; the Mongols in the 1200s) were relatively few and far-between. Rather than being subject to numerous sudden, destructive invasions, Europe was populated by the slow migration of farming folk (Germans and Slavs) from western Asia *north* of the steppe belt.

Another unique feature that is visible from the map is that Europe is a *peninsula of peninsulas*. The Crimea, Turkey, Greece, Italy, Portugal/Spain ("Iberia"), Brittany, Scandinavia: all are landmasses reaching into the sea. Even the British Isles were an extension of France until "the Channel" filled with melting ice at the last glacial retreat. This "peninsular" layout combined with mountain ranges and rivers running in almost every direction to **isolate** Europe from the Asian steppe as well as to **break up** Europe into "pockets" of rich farm land attractive to settlers and migrants coming west from Asia. Also, notice its *position*: Europe is situated *north* of the great steppe belt, closer to the Arctic Circle and the North Atlantic; this meant a colder, wetter climate (more snow and rain), a habitat hostile to tropical diseases (linked to parasites like hookworms). Although Europe would suffer its share of epidemics throughout its history (the "Black Plague" of the 1340s is the most infamous), *compared to Asia* such outbreaks were less common and less deadly.

Despite its small size compared to Asia, Europe developed a more intensive and *diverse* **agriculture**, making use of a wider variety of soils, forests, and animals (some of which were brought from western Asia). Local economies thrived, producing surpluses for trade with nearby communities boasting a variety of products. Unlike Asia, where long-distance **trade** was measured in *thousands* of miles over nomad-infested steppes and deserts, Europe's trade routes were measured in *hundreds* of miles at most, enjoyed easy river[5] as well as seacoast transport, and (as mentioned above) was less vulnerable to nomad incursion. Again, despite its smaller area, Europe never fell under the sway of a single imperial state for more than a few years[6] and never has *all* of Europe been so ruled. Instead, following in the tradition of the ancient Greek and medieval Italian "city-states," Europe evolved as a collection of *"nation-states,"* culturally and religiously unified but politically and linguistically divided. This led to a unique European **mentality** in which *international competition* drove **trade**, new technologies, and a thirst for new information and ideas. And this "thirst for the new" not only made possible the great American discoveries of the 1500s, but also helped spark an inner transformation of Europe itself.

The Rise of the Western "Mentality"

Much longer books than this one have been written on the many facets of Western culture and "**mentality**." Beginning with ancient Greek art, literature, and philosophy, it developed through Roman law and technology, medieval feudal political and religious institutions, and on to the "Renaissance," the "Reformation," the American discoveries, the "Scientific Revolution," and the "Enlightenment." I suspect that, for many of you, these are labels, meaningless "tags" you are asked to memorize without understanding why. I will not attempt to explain them all here. For the purposes of this *Student's Guide*, I want you to first look at the **"5 Foundations"** again, and connect **The Rise of the West** with Foundations 3 and 4: **Nationalism & Democracy** and **Industrialization & Capitalism.** You will want to keep this in mind as a landmark on the horizon (like a church steeple or a mountain range), as you proceed through the rest of this chapter. You will not get lost as long as you know where you are in relation to the "Washington Monument" or the "Eiffel Tower."

---

[5] Most of Asia's rivers flow on a north–south axis (the Don, Dnieper, Volga, Amu Darya and Sir Darya), thus, "against the grain" of east–west trade between Europe and India or China. This hampered east-west wagon-borne trade across Asia, while hardly hindering horse-nomads.

[6] Rome came close before 500 CE; two "Charles's"—Charlemagne in the 700s CE and Charles V in the early 1500s; Napoleon in the early 1800s; and Hitler's "Third Reich" in the 1940s.

Cultural Revolution

After about 1500 CE, at a time when most Asian states and empires had settled into a pattern of striving to preserve their diverse established traditions (authoritarian political structures, confiscatory tax/economic policies, and religious/philosophical systems that discouraged change and speculative thought or innovation), Europe, never a particularly quiet place, experienced several centuries of political, economic, cultural, and religious **upheaval** that had no parallel in the rest of the world. This is best sampled by looking at four men whose actions and ideas in the span of about 250 years helped to "stir the pot" and created the modern Western mindset. In their separate realms of interest (and with assistance from many others), these four paved the way for **Foundations 3 & 4** (and, ultimately, **5** as well).

But before we start, there is one more thing to keep in mind: the *intellectual effects* of **Foundation 1, the Columbian Exchange.** Think about it: The news that two *new continents* had been found, full of unknown plants, animals, and peoples, was itself astounding to a culture that had convinced itself that it knew what "the world" was: Europe, Africa, and Asia. And they had barely begun familiarizing themselves with those three continents. Europe was a predominantly Christian society; the Bible did not mention these new places, and the place of the Native Americans in "God's Order" was unclear. Finally, if Europeans were *that* ignorant about the basic structure of the world, *what else* did they not know? For the "traditional" societies of the "East," these questions were not so pressing. (They also had, as we saw, no access to the Americas, so the new lands did not factor into their mindset.) The Europeans were *curious,* almost desperately so. They lived in a subcontinent land-locked by "empty" oceans, impassable deserts, and hostile Muslim empires. The discovery of the Americas was a massive "breakout" moment, a "game changer," as if, in football, one team "discovered" a third end zone that the other team could not see. America was "the pot of gold at the end of the rainbow," but it raised only more questions: could there be *other* pots of gold? *Other* rainbows?

What if everything they had taught themselves to believe was **wrong**?

Aside from this "cosmic" question, many primary institutions of western European society were breaking down or transforming into something else in this period (14th to 16th centuries):

Institutional Breakdown

- **Political** change: The traditional power structure (kings and landed noblemen) supported by the **religious** authority of the Roman Catholic Church was *fading*, and soon would be overturned by the revolutions of the 18th and 19th centuries;
- **Economic** change: Wealth traditionally held in land ("real" estate = immovable) by kings, the noble elite, and their knight retainers was *weakening* in the face of a new system based on the movement of *money and credit* largely controlled by merchants, bankers, and shippers (soon to be called "**capitalists**").
- **Social** change: Previously, peasants, artisans, and merchants had been held down, taxed, exploited, and otherwise ignored. But this was *changing*; Europe's "basket" of kingdoms and principalities (over 300 in Germany!) meant that many people were able to move around seeking new opportunities. Merchants in particular extended *credit* to kings and nobles *in exchange for* the right to govern/make law for themselves. They could even protect themselves by buying or renting armies and navies for money, rather than depend on the king's levies.

From Merriam-Webster's Collegiate® Dictionary, 11th Edition ©2016 by Merriam-Webster, Inc. (www.Merriam-Webster.com)

By 1500, Europe was slowly leaving its "feudal" era behind: cities, commerce, and literacy were rising; education was more widely available; the printing press was invented in the 1460s,[7] so not only the Bible but potentially *anything* could be *mass-produced* for a widening reading public. This technological breakthrough is now viewed as the most important factor in the success of the Protestant Reformation, to which we now turn.

"Here I stand . . ."

If Christopher Columbus can be seen as a "revolutionary" figure because of what his actions set in motion (much of which he certainly did not foresee or intend), then Martin Luther belongs in the same category. He was very much

---

[7] It is now acknowledged that the Chinese beat Gutenberg to it by over 200 years, but it seems that Europeans were unaware of the Chinese invention, and came up with it independently. Also, the alphabet made learning to read much easier than the thousands of characters of written Chinese. Thus, the press was more useful to Europeans.

a product of early 16th century German-speaking Europe. He aspired to join the rising "middle class" of paid professionals, by studying to become a lawyer. A devout Roman Catholic, he nevertheless had no plans of joining the clergy, let alone of launching a revolt against it. But because of a frightening encounter with a thunderstorm, he promised God he would become a monk, and he kept that promise. He joined a local monastery, where he dedicated himself feverishly to winning "favor" with God.[8] After years of struggle, he discovered in the writings of St. Paul the liberating declaration that "the just shall live by faith," which to Luther (and most Protestant Christians today) meant that trying to win God's favor by one's own effort ("works") was useless, when all God asked in exchange for forgiveness of sins and "salvation" was simple faith and trust.

It probably seems strange that this wholly religious insight could be the basis of a transformative mass movement, but it was Luther, exploring the implications of this teaching (salvation by faith alone), realized that the Roman Catholic Church had been teaching the opposite (salvation by works) for centuries; that its primary function (so it seemed to him) was to teach that one had to "earn salvation," by obeying the Church without question, and by performing the various rituals and pilgrimages it called for. What offended Luther was a fund-raising campaign authorized by the pope in Rome, intended to finance the building of St. Peter's Basilica. In order to encourage voluntary donations, the pope granted forgiveness of sins to the living and release from "Purgatory" for the dead ("plenary indulgence") to anyone who gave money. To Luther, this was nothing short of *heresy*, and he composed a long diatribe against it (the "95 Theses"). With this publication (in its way, a forerunner of the American *Declaration of Independence*), the so-called **Protestant Reformation** began.

Martin Luther (1483–1546). Engraved by C. E. Wagstaff and Published in The Gallery of Portraits with Memoirs Encyclopedia, United Kingdom, 1833.

Kateryna Kon/Shutterstock.com

---

[8] The best known biography of Luther is still Roland Bainton's *Here I Stand: A Life of Martin Luther* (Abingdon reprint, 2013).

St. Peter's Basilica, Vatican, Rome.

Definition of heresy
plural: heresies

    1a **:** adherence to a religious opinion contrary to church dogma

    b **:** denial of a revealed truth by a baptized member of the Roman Catholic Church

    c **:** an opinion or doctrine contrary to church dogma

    2a **:** dissent or deviation from a dominant theory, opinion, or practice

    b **:** an opinion, doctrine, or practice contrary to the truth or to generally accepted beliefs or standards

From Merriam-Webster's Collegiate® Dictionary, 11th Edition ©2016 by Merriam-Webster, Inc. (www.Merriam-Webster.com)

    This is not the proper place to explore what happened afterward; what's crucial here is to observe *why* this religious rebellion against the pope's authority changed the future of the Western world. Notice that here in Europe, unlike in Asia, religion could be a *force for change.*

    First, Luther's revolt asserted the **primacy of Scripture** (the Bible) over the Church's authority. For about 1200 years, the Church had "owned" the "Holy Scriptures," having originally collected the various Jewish and Christian writings into a single volume[9] and then declaring this collection "canon," meaning it would be the basis for all belief and practice in the Church; but the Church (its priests, officials, and scholars) reserved the right to *interpret* what the Bible said. By Luther's time, this meant that very few people (literate or not) ever saw a Bible, or dared to read it for themselves; they went along with what their priest or bishop *told them* it said. Luther completely shattered this tradition of Church authority by declaring that the Bible was meant for all people, and all should be able to read it *and interpret it for themselves.* Luther "made it real" by going much further: A scholar himself, he *translated* the Bible from its original surviving Hebrew and Greek manuscripts into German, his local language. This meant that any person, who could read, could read the Bible (and those who could not, could probably find someone to read it *to* them).[10]

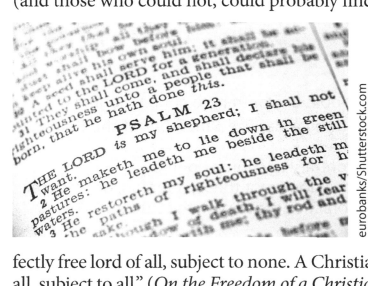
eurobanks/Shutterstock.com

If Luther had done nothing else, he would have a prominent place in the history books. But we are not finished with him yet. His doctrine that that each individual Christian was responsible to God alone and hence did not need a priest to forgive his sins was a tremendously liberating idea. Luther wrote: "A Christian is a perfectly free lord of all, subject to none. A Christian is a perfectly dutiful servant of all, subject to all." (*On the Freedom of a Christian,* 1520). This was the first argument for the *liberty of conscience* in Western history, and was a powerful step toward **Democracy,** the idea that authority (political or religious) comes from God and is directed through individuals to delegated "governors," *not* handed down to rulers who then ruled over everyone in the name of God. It appears from his writings that Luther himself was not fully aware of the implications of

---

[9] What we call a "book" (a stack of uniform paper/papyrus sheets attached on one side for easy "flipping") was originally called a "codex" to distinguish it from the scrolls that had been in use; "bible" comes from "Byblos," the town in Lebanon where the codex first appeared. It is now believed that the Jewish-Christian scriptures were among the first (if not *the* first) "things from Byblos" to appear in the Roman world; hence "*the* Bible."

[10] Believe it or not, people gathered to hear the Bible read and to discuss it, where it was most convenient for people to gather: in bars and alehouses.

his teaching:[11] that by questioning the authority of the Church over the individual conscience, he was opening a door to questioning *all* forms of established authority over the individual; and that the future would see individuals challenge authority by appealing to a *document* (the Bible, or in our time, the U.S. Constitution) to assert their "God-given rights." As we will see in the next chapter, this *revolution*ary idea (pun intended) would transform government from an instrument to keep order in society into one that protects individual rights. Like Columbus, Luther unwittingly opened a door that others passed through, and accelerated **The Rise of the West.**

The "Enlightenment" (1600s–1700s)

The next stage in the transformation of Western thought and culture began in the wake of terrible "Religious Wars" set off by Luther's revolt against the Roman Catholic Church. Immediately, every Christian in Europe ("Western Christendom") was confronted with a choice: to embrace **Protestantism**, or reject it? (See definition.)

Definition of protestant

> *capitalized* ***a*** : any of a group of German princes and cities presenting a defense of freedom of conscience against an edict of the Diet of Spires in 1529 intended to suppress the Lutheran movement
> ***b*** : a member of any of several church denominations denying the universal authority of the Pope and affirming the Reformation principles of justification by faith alone, the priesthood of all believers, and the primacy of the Bible as the only source of revealed truth; *broadly* : a Christian not of a Catholic or Eastern church

From Merriam-Webster's Collegiate® Dictionary, 11th Edition ©2016 by Merriam-Webster, Inc. (www.Merriam-Webster.com)

Those in political authority chose sides too, most often based on non-religious factors. Most of Germany sided with Luther against the pope out of resentment of Church taxes spent in Rome; thus, Luther also qualifies as an early

---

[11] Luther, infamously, denounced German peasants who rose up against their landlords and creditors by citing his teachings in support. He insisted that all should obey established political and economic authority.

apostle of **Nationalism** (see next chapter). These disagreements over Church authority and the right to interpret Scripture descended into communal and international violence. By the early 1600s, many educated men were disgusted by the unrest and atrocities tied to religious disagreements, and began to call for a calmer, more rational approach to addressing issues of the day.

From this spirit arose what was called by later writers "the Enlightenment," which can be **defined** as an *intellectual movement that critiqued existing government, society and economic development by appealing to* **reason** *as the proper path to human happiness.* Not anti-religion as such, the Enlightenment thinkers did insist that appeals to Scripture (and conscience) had one supreme drawback: They were "subjective" truth; in other words, one person's "truth" was another's falsehood. It could not be proven or disproven; it is a matter of opinion. What was needed was a focus on *objective* truth: What can be agreed upon by all (or most) people, based on sense observation ("empiricism") interpreted *rationally.* (Simply put, we must all agree that 2 + 2 = 4, and that the sun rises in the east, regardless of *why* these things are so. A Christian and an atheist can at least agree this far.) The Enlightenment thinkers took this as the starting point for their writings.

When we speak of the "Enlightenment," we are talking about hundreds of men and women from all over Europe. Many, if not most, belonged to the landed aristocracy; what this meant was that they were formally educated and wealthy enough to pursue their interests: literary, scientific, economic, and so on. They could pay a printer to publish their work; they enjoyed gathering at stylish parties where they could, eat, drink, and talk about their ideas. Many upper-class women would join in, often hosting these gatherings as a way to pursue *their* intellectual interests; with little formal education allowed for women at this time, this was the only way a woman could hope to learn anything. (Imagine partying with your professors!) Out of the hundreds of people involved, I have chosen just **three** whom I feel were the pre-eminent minds in three important areas of thought, whose writings form the core of **The Rise of the West.** It happens that all three came from the British Isles, an indication perhaps of the leading role Britain would soon play in Western expansion. The first two point toward the development of **Foundation 3;** the last one fits properly into **Foundation 4.**

Isaac Newton (1642–1727)

Often considered the "Father of the Enlightenment," this influential Englishman is best known for a book he published in Latin[12] in 1687: *Principia Mathematica*. It was a mathematical proof of the astronomical observations of earlier scientists like Nicolas Copernicus and Galileo Galilei. His arguments laid the groundwork for modern physics, and his assumptions remained unquestioned until the 20th century writings of Albert Einstein and Stephen Hawking. However, Newton's real (and, again, unintended) contribution was not to *physical* science, but to *political* science: Newton proposed a model of the Universe that rested on the basis of certain fundamental "Natural Laws of Motion" that God Himself had employed to create all the matter and energy that composed "reality."

Isaac Newton (1643–1727). Engraved by E.Scriven and published in The Gallery Of Portraits With Memoirs encyclopedia, United Kingdom, 1837.

Georgios Kollidas/Shutterstock.com

Very interesting, as far as it goes, except that this one notion ("Natural Law") struck at the basis of Roman Catholic Church teaching for hundreds of years: that God directly controlled everything that happened, from the motions of the planets in the sky right down to who the ruler of the kingdom was. (It helped that England had left the Catholic Church for good in the 1560s, and the King's authority rested on a "homemade" Anglican Church establishment that crowned him. Thus Newton was not suppressed as Copernicus and Galileo had been.) And here is where the "political science" comes in: the implication was that God, far from "micro-managing" everything, preferred to let the "Laws of Nature" run their course. So, instead of a specially-chosen "Divine Right" monarch, the person on the throne was actually . . . just a humble human, born into a particular family.

---

[12] Latin was the international language of learning until the 19tht century. Anyone educated in a European university was fluent (or at least literate) in Latin. This meant that the widest possible (educated) audience could get your ideas. Today you most likely cannot read a book written in Italian or German; you would have to learn that language to research and write in it (as I had to learn German to research German history).

This insight raised an even scarier question: If political authority (the right to "rule") did not come directly from God, where *did* it come from? By what "Right" (obviously not "Divine") did anyone claim rulership over *anyone*? (Of course, *someone* has to be in charge; this was never seriously questioned; the issue was: How do you determine who that person or persons should be?) Another Englishman who had read and pondered Newton's book provided an answer that is still the philosophical basis for most Western governments today.

John Locke (1632–1704)

In 1688, England's King James II was overthrown by Parliament and replaced by Stadtholder William of the Netherlands and his wife Mary, James's eldest daughter, in what would be described today as a *coup d'état* (sudden seizure of power). This event is called the "Glorious Revolution" in England (because it was successful *and* almost bloodless). Although England remained a monarchy, the new "duarchy" of William III and Mary II accepted the throne with a major concession: they would "reign" while Parliament "ruled." In other words, they would be expected to run England as a sort of "supreme executive," responsible to the elected members of the House of Commons and the hereditary House of Lords, both bodies "representative" of the English people as a whole (or, at least, the property-holding segment of it). Now, by modern standards, this would seem little more than a change of management in a corporation; but it truly was a "glorious revolution" in this sense: Parliament (the people's representatives assembled) had asserted its authority against the monarch, and had "fired" and replaced him. And not only did the new monarchs go along; they more or less willingly agreed with Parliament's "right" to do so *again* if it saw fit. Indeed, the "Revolution" was crowned in 1689 by the adoption of a "Bill of Rights" that guaranteed every Englishman's freedom from summary execution, arbitrary arrest, or seizure of property without a court ruling ("due process of law"). This ended almost 50 years of political and social upheaval that had involved civil war, "regicide" (the trial and execution of King James's father, Charles I), military dictatorship under Oliver Cromwell, and finally the Restoration of the monarchy under King James's older brother, Charles II. Then, James II challenged Parliament's authority, and lost.

An interested observer of these momentous events was John Locke. He was a "political philosopher" who had developed his ideas before the Glorious Revolution, but his best-known work in this area appeared in 1689 as *Two Treatises of Government.* It argued that the only valid basis for government is *consent of the governed* based on "Natural Rights" of life, liberty, and property under the *rule of law.* So government, rather than gaining its power from God, instead was granted it by the *governed*; and further, that if "the people" find themselves in danger from "Arbitrary Power," they have the *right to rebel*, and thus to "resume their original Liberty." Locke thus gave a philosophical and political foundation for **Democracy**, as well as opened the door to the revolutionary upheavals of the 1770s–1790s in Britain's American colonies and in France. Indeed, Thomas Jefferson's *Declaration of Independence* is largely a "hymn" to John Locke, whose famous phrase he altered to "life, liberty, and the pursuit of happiness."

John Locke (1632–1704). Engraved by J. Pofselwhite and published in The Gallery Of Portraits With Memoirs encyclopedia, United Kingdom, 1836.

Georgios Kollidas/Shutterstock.com

Adam Smith (1712–1790)

The third person I want to draw your attention to was a Scotsman of a later generation, who grew up in a newly-minted nation called the United Kingdom of Great Britain. His homeland, Scotland, had been formally joined to England to form "the UK," and he was one of a number of Scots who used the union to advance their ideas and ambitions; this is often spoken of as the "Scottish Enlightenment." The gentleman in question is still the single most influential economic thinker and writer in history: Adam Smith.

Adam Smith (1723–1790)

Everett Historical/Shutterstock.com

Smith is best known for publishing in 1776 a book called *The Wealth of Nations*, in which he launches a withering attack on the prevailing economic theory of the day, *mercantilism.*

As the text box explains, mercantilism was the idea that a country's government (king and parliament) reserved the right to tightly control the national economy, mainly by **(1)** *maximizing exports* and *minimizing imports* so as to keep *specie* (gold and silver) at home as much as possible, and **(2)** granting royal *monopolies* to companies or individuals who bid for the privilege; they

---

Definition of Mercantilism

1: the theory or practice of mercantile pursuits : commercialism

2: an economic system developing during the decay of feudalism to unify and increase the power and especially the monetary wealth of a nation by a strict governmental regulation of the entire national economy usually through policies designed to secure an accumulation of bullion, a favorable balance of trade, the development of agriculture and manufactures, and the establishment of foreign trading monopolies.

From Merriam-Webster's Collegiate® Dictionary, 11th Edition ©2016 by Merriam-Webster, Inc. (www.Merriam-Webster.com)

---

could then control the trade in a particular commodity (for instance, the East India Company enjoyed the exclusive right to bring tea into the American colonies; you may recall a protest in Boston in 1773 about this) and charge whatever they liked for it.

Full Definition of monopoly
plural: monopolies

1: exclusive ownership through legal privilege, command of supply, or concerted action

2: exclusive possession or control

3: a commodity controlled by one party

4: one that has a monopoly

From Merriam-Webster's Collegiate® Dictionary, 11th Edition ©2016 by Merriam-Webster, Inc. (www.Merriam-Webster.com)

Smith, as an "enlightened" (rational) thinker, thought this practice was "irrational." **First**, the practice of squeezing imports and encouraging exports (assuming all nations did so, which most of them did) only meant that little trade was done; with everyone trying to sell and trying to avoid buying, commerce suffered. **Second**, granting exclusive monopolies limited supply and kept prices artificially high (since the monopoly company charged what it liked)[13]. Additionally, the home consumer suffered from avoidable scarcity and artificially high prices. The upshot was that the consumer lost by not getting the goods he wanted, in the quality he wanted, because the supplies were low and the prices high; even the monopoly company suffered, because it could not sell to the consumer the quantities he wanted; therefore, it missed out on higher profits in the name of avoiding competition. Then there was the bid (really a bribe) the company had to pay the government as the "cost of doing business."

Smith proposed a solution based on what he perceived as the "Natural Law of Markets": allow the exchange of goods and services to be governed by a "free market" ruled by "supply and demand." In such a system (with the government remaining a largely disinterested observer, only intervening when a crime was committed or a legal complaint filed), prices and wages would "float" more or less freely, rising and falling with the fluctuations of supply and demand. Smith described as a "hidden hand" the gravitational forces of the market. Put most simply, if a commodity was rare and a lot of people wanted it, the price would rise; but the scarcity would then be cured by the "hidden hand": people would strive to produce and supply more of that commodity in order to profit from the high price. But then, as supply rose to meet demand, the "hidden hand" would again gently intervene, and the demand (and price) would fall to its "natural" level, and remain there until another shift in supply and/or demand nudged the price up (or down) again.

---

[13] Hence the "Boston Tea Party": The East India Company and the British government colluded by importing cheap tea into Boston with a small tax attached to the price; the colonists "smelled a rat" and decided to avoid paying the tax by dumping the tea into the harbor.

> **Simple Definition of free market**
>
> **1:** an economic market or system in which prices are based on competition among private businesses and not controlled by a government
>
> From Merriam-Webster's Collegiate® Dictionary, 11th Edition ©2016 by Merriam-Webster, Inc. (www.Merriam-Webster.com)

Smith's ideas took a while to take hold; old habits die hard, even in "forward-looking" Western Europe. It is ironic how (as we have seen) European states were in such dire competition for resources, power, control over trade routes, and so on. Yet Smith had to point out to them (not just the British!) that *increased competition* would benefit *everyone*: the consumer/buyer would get as much of whatever they liked, at a "**reasonable**" price; while the seller (even though forced to compete with other producers by lowering his price) would *make more profit by selling more* to the market.

Smith's ideas (together with Locke's promotion of private property rights) would pave the way for the West's economic transformation of itself and the entire world: the 19th century's twin economic achievements: The **Industrial Revolution & Capitalism.**

CONCLUSION

The Rise of the West is responsible for the fundamental institutions and practices that govern your individual life today, and that of billions of people around the world. It characterizes "the way things are" and its global power is seen today as an instrument of continuity and authority. In politics, economics, education, culture, science, and technology, its reach is irresistible. The last time in history a single civilizational outlook was so dominant over so much of the world was the "Hellenistic period" (300s BCE to 700s CE), in which Greek language, art, and social and political values ruled from Spain to India, molding and transforming (sometimes replacing) older social and cultural patterns. Even so, **The Rise of the West** has been an aggressive engine of change (often violent) in our world up to this very moment.

I'd like to end this chapter with a look ahead at the links between **Foundation 2** and the last three.

- The *Reformation* was, at its heart, a revolt against *priests* (a struggle for *religious* liberty).
- The late 18th century *Atlantic Revolutions* (American and French) were a revolt against rule by *kings* and *nobles* (a struggle for *political* and *social* liberty).
- The 20th century *Socialist Revolutions* (Russian and Chinese, among others) were a revolt against the power of *capitalists* (a struggle for *economic* liberty).
- *All* fostered the creation of *national states* & promised increased **Democracy (Foundation 3)**.
- *All* paved the way for ***Industrialization* (Foundation 4).**
- *All* spread & sped *globally* **(Foundation 5)**.

From Merriam-Webster's Collegiate® Dictionary, 11th Edition ©2016 by Merriam-Webster, Inc. (www.Merriam-Webster.com)

THINKING IN TIME

Find a copy of the U.S. Constitution and read it carefully. How many elements of the Reformation and Enlightenment can you find in its clauses? How influential on your life and in your nation's life are these ideas? If you were born in or have visited another country, how many of these concepts can you discover in that nation's life?

_____

_____

_____

_____

_____

_____

_____

_____

_____

_____

_____

_____

_____

_____

_____

_____

_____

_____

_____

_____

_____

_____

_____

FOUNDATION 3

NATIONALISM & DEMOCRACY

The Columbian
Exchange

Globalization and
Acceleration

The Rise of
the West

Industrialization and
Capitalism

Nationalism and
Democracy

Dulce et decorum est pro patria mori
("It is sweet and glorious to die for one's country.")

—Horace, *Odes*

Those who die for their country are martyrs
and those who live for their country are greater martyrs.

—Bhagat Puran Singh

. . . that this nation, under God, shall have a new birth of freedom
-- and that government of the people, by the people, for the people,
shall not perish from the earth.

—Abraham Lincoln, "Gettysburg Address," 1863

The third **Foundation of the Modern World** consists of two paired political ideas that are among the most powerful forces working in the world today. I have paired them because I see them as nearly inseparable. Although there have been and still are countries where fervent patriotism is not combined with a popular government, history shows that such regimes are unstable and short-lived. In the long run, you cannot demand that people sacrifice for a political system that grants little in return. Such governments are usually overthrown, eventually. However, governments can maintain popular support by granting a say in how the society is governed, and who governs it.

The marriage between **Nationalism & Democracy** is as old as the "West" itself. It first appeared in ancient Greece, among the city-state (*polis*) culture. It is common knowledge that the Greeks "invented" **Democracy**, in the sense that they elected their lawgivers and debated issues openly before voting on them. But what is often missed is

Gilmanshin/Shutterstock.com

Pericles of Athens, Ancient Greek statesman

the "other side of the coin": the fact that those in the particular city-state who were permitted to vote (free, adult male landowners who also served in the *phalanx* or volunteer militia) felt a deep and fierce sense of loyalty to their *polis*, and were ready to die to defend its freedom if necessary (**Nationalism**). **Democracy** worked well in a small, self-governing city-state, but failed in the era of large "universal" empires like Rome. This legacy was kept alive by cultures that admired the Greeks; when monarchy began to come under attack in the 18th century, **Democracy** in some form became a possible alternative authority system (see previous chapter).

Nationalism & Democracy was reborn in the American colonies of Great Britain. In this sense, we can see the **Columbian Exchange** at work again. Transplanted Europeans of (mostly) British stock confronted a wilderness populated by forests and Indians and tried to re-create the political and social order they had enjoyed back home, including a landed aristocracy (tobacco planters in Virginia), a peasant labor force (African slaves and European indentured servants), and a "middle class" of artisans, ship owners, and educated professionals (doctors, lawyers, businessmen). In Europe, all was held together by hereditary monarchy (guided in England by an elected Parliament). But in the colonies, no king was present; no military establishment was on hand to maintain order or defend the colonists. Most of the time, the colonists had to fend for themselves. Back in Europe, most farm land was owned or controlled by a hereditary aristocracy; in America, unexplored acres of woodland, with a river system just beyond, beckoned to anyone who dared to seek out and settle in. In short, "social control" was the order of the day in Europe; in America, it was nearly impossible. (Notice the role of **Geography** here.) As a result, under British protection, the American colonies evolved into a collection of 17th and 18th century "city-states": they were scattered across over two thousand miles of sea coast from Massachusetts to Georgia; and they were largely self-governing.

The story of the American Revolution is too familiar to repeat here; what I will do is point to the *global causes and effects* of the American uprising (**Globalization**). First, the Revolution arose out of a squabble over tax and trade policy between the colonies and the British government. The colonists were frustrated by the *Mercantilism* that Adam Smith attacked in the

Wealth of Nations. Second, the "Glorious Revolution" was an inspiration to the colonists, as were the writings of Locke. So when the British government proposed to raise revenue by changing the customary procedure (taxing the colonists directly rather than through their locally elected legislatures), the colonists felt their "Natural Rights" had been violated, and rebelled (as Locke had told them they had a right to do). The result by 1790 was a new **National** government for the Americans, founded upon **Democratic** principles. This proved in turn to be an inspiration both to French, Spanish, and Portuguese colonists in the Americas (all of whom rebelled and won independence in the early 1800s), but also to the French, who rebelled against and toppled King Louis XVI in the 1790s. What resulted in France was a government based upon an elected **National** Assembly and a *Declaration of the Rights of Man and the Citizen* proclaiming **Democratic** principles.

The success of this "Atlantic Revolution" further transformed the West and the world. The bells of **Nationalism & Democracy** continue to peal around the world today. In your lifetime, they ended Soviet Russian domination of Eastern Europe (after 1989), dissolved the Soviet Union itself into separate **national** states (although **Democracy** and the "rule of law" have not yet fully established themselves), and in the Middle East after 2011, a series of uprisings against authoritarian regimes (the so-called "Arab Spring") has destabilized the entire region. **National** states like Iraq and Syria are fracturing along ethnic and sectarian lines, but what drives a lot of the turmoil is a popular struggle for "self-determination," a government controlled by the *People*—**Democracy**.

Nationalism

Historian Hans Kohn has defined **Nationalism** as "a state of mind in which the individual feels that everyone owes his supreme secular loyalty to the nation-state."[1] This is a very economical definition that rewards "unpacking."

---

[1] "Nationalism," *Encyclopedia Britannica* 15th ed., 1979.

> **Nationalism:** *a state of mind in which the individual feels that everyone owes his supreme secular loyalty to the nation-state.*
>
> From Merriam-Webster's Collegiate® Dictionary, 11th Edition ©2016 by Merriam-Webster, Inc. (www.Merriam-Webster.com)

Stated most briefly, this means that people are persuaded that each person should be most loyal and ready to sacrifice (under/next to God) to their country, and that they believe that *everyone else* should hold this same attitude. Each of you probably remembers "pledging to the flag" at school; in addition, sports contests (even concerts, like one I attended recently) begin with a salute to the flag or the playing of the National Anthem. All of this reinforces the sense of reverence for the **nation**. But in earlier times, there were overlapping and competing loyalties: to tribe, clan, ethnic group, social class, landlord, family, and religious sect. **Nationalism** is actually a very recent invention, and one that coincides with the appearance of the "**nation-state**."

Another prominent historian, Eric Hobsbawm, defines the national-state (or "national state" or just "nation") this way:

> "The characteristic modern state . . . is a
>
> • *territorially coherent and unbroken area with sharply defined frontiers,*
> • *governed by a single sovereign authority and*
> • *according to a single fundamental system of administration and law."*[2]
>
> From Merriam-Webster's Collegiate® Dictionary, 11th Edition ©2016 by Merriam-Webster, Inc. (www.Merriam-Webster.com)

As you can see, there are three criteria for a national state: *geographical, political,* and *legal.* First, a modern national state can be said to exist in a *physical* sense; as you are reading this book, written by an American for American students, you most likely are reading this in the United States, not in France. (Although, if you are *not* reading this in the United States, I'd love to hear from you!) You can tell where a particular country is by simply looking at a map or globe. Here is a political map of Europe:

---

[2] Eric Hobsbawm, *The Age of Revolution* (Barnes & Noble, 1996), 88. Bullet points are mine. See also his *Nations and Nationalism since 1780* (Canto/Cambridge, Univ. Press, 2005), pp. 80 ff.

B. BELGIUM
B.H. BOSNIA AND HERZEGOVINA
D. DENMARK
E. ESTONIA
L. LUXEMBOURG
MAC. MACEDONIA
MOL. MOLDOVA
M. MONTENEGRO
N. NETHERLANDS
SL. SLOVENIA
S. SWITZERLAND

Pyty/Shutterstock.com

Although you can't see boundaries from space, they are physically real, as real as a mountain range. Governments want you to know when you are about to enter their country, because you will then be under their *jurisdiction* (literally "law-speak," legal authority). This sign is telling you that you are about to enter Germany, a member state of the European Union:

So countries exist *physically* because you cannot be in Canada if you are in Mexico. Japan and China are close to each other, but cannot be mistaken as the same country.

defotoberg/Shutterstock.com

Hobsbawm says that a nation exists in a *political* sense, too. In other words, each nation has but one "sovereign" (supreme) government ruling over it. It is established in international law and custom that *only* the United States Government makes and enforces law inside the territory of the United States. It does not (and cannot) do so anywhere else, such as Canada or Thailand. No other country can make or enforce law in the United States; nor can any other "authority," such as the State of Texas or Apple Corporation or the United Methodist Church or the National Football League. Now, U.S. law is enforced over all of these organizations (for instance, Apple must pay its employees the national minimum wage); but in no sense can these organizations "make law" applying to every American citizen. The State of Texas is permitted to make law for Texans, *provided that* such laws do not clash with or violate Federal law. (For instance, Texas can set a higher minimum wage if it wishes, but cannot set one *lower* than that established by the U.S. Government.)

Finally, a "nation" has a single *administrative and legal system.* What this means is that there is only one *system* of government (Texas has no king, merely a governor; each of the 50 states has a governor and an elected legislature) and one legal *system* (if accused of a crime, you will be "processed" in a manner consistent across the nation, whether you were arrested in southern Poland or eastern Poland, and will be prosecuted according to practices recognized and employed regardless of where in the country you are, and (theoretically) regardless of your socio-economic status, gender or political affiliation). Most countries have a version of our Supreme Court, which has final *jurisdiction* over legal cases involving individual rights under the Constitution; one can appeal from a lower (county, circuit, state or Federal) court to the Supreme Court, but you cannot appeal *beyond* it, to the International Court at the Hague, for instance, unless you are accused of an *international* crime (genocide, for example).

You may be wondering why all of this matters. Simply because none of this was true 200 years ago. There were many countries without "coherent and unbroken" frontiers recognized by all other nations.

Think about this: Does the United States meet Hobsbawm's standard of "a territorially coherent and unbroken area with sharply defined frontiers"?

From Merriam-Webster's Collegiate® Dictionary, 11th Edition ©2016 by Merriam-Webster, Inc. (www.Merriam-Webster.com)

boreala/Shutterstock.com

Do you see Hawaii?

There was once a Kingdom of Prussia that stretched across northern Germany, pieces of it separated by other principalities. As for "sovereign" governing authority, in many regions in Europe the king's authority was hemmed in by locally elected bodies (*parlements* in France) that actually ratified (approved and enforced) his decrees—or not. There was also the Roman Catholic Church, whose pronouncements were considered to be "law" over all of Christendom, regardless of what a king thought of them.[3] Lastly, many kingdoms had overlapping legal authorities, independent courts and court systems; the Roman Catholic Church had its own legal

---

[3] This is why Henry VIII took England out of the Catholic Church when the pope would not grant him a divorce. Parliament then granted an "Act of Supremacy" making his will sovereign in religious matters, creating an English church and making him England's "pope."

system for processing priests and monks accused of crime. (The military retains this privilege today by handling service people accused of crime by recourse to "Military Justice.")

All of this was swept away after the 1790s. But before we examine the changes to **Nationalism** brought about by the Revolutions, we must briefly look at 17th and 18th century trends that were strengthening it before 1776. First, "Absolutist" kings like Louis XIV of France and Peter the Great of Russia were successful in breaking down many of the older, local ties that bound peasant to landlord as well as Church (Louis did not go as far as Henry VIII but accomplished the same ends by asserting his authority over the Catholic Church in France, not least by expelling the Protestant "Huguenots"; Peter asserted his authority over the Russian Orthodox Church). Both determined to increasingly tie the population's loyalty to their royal persons, as living embodiments of the kingdom. Louis is remembered for saying *"L'Etat, c'est moi."* ("I am the state.") If anything, this represented **Nationalism** without **Democracy,** an increase in the power of the national state, but with the state's authority still vested in a hereditary monarch backed by religious authority.

As "states" became increasingly "national" in appearance and behavior, changes were necessary in how they interacted with each other and with their populations. In 1618, Protestant and Catholic states went to war with each other; this soon developed into a "free for all" that had nothing to do with the Reformation at all (Catholic states allied with Protestant states against other Catholic states) and it ended in 1648 in mutual exhaustion, several million dead, and "Germany" in ruins (everyone had used it as a battlefield, since there was no German state at the time). As they would again in 1815, 1919, and 1945, representatives of the warring powers met at the German town of Westphalia to try to restore and maintain peace and order, and created the modern European "states system." It had two components that still hold true today: *internal* and *external.*

- **External relations:** At the Peace of Westphalia in 1648, the monarchies agreed for the first time to draw lines on the map clearly demarcating where one "nation" ended and another began, and then agreed to respect others' "territorial integrity" (boundaries) and sovereignty (each government's right to rule its territory); in effect, "keep your hands to yourself." In law, this meant that to cross another's boundary in force was an "act of war" that justified an armed response. This was the beginning of a concept of "international law" (rules binding on all nations) that still persists today, and culminated in the United Nations Organization.

- **Internal Affairs:** Also at Westphalia, it was mutually agreed that what went on in one nation was no business of another, and that each nation's government had absolute claim (and right to coerce) its own residents' or subjects' support in the form of taxes, mandatory military service, and obedience to its laws. This was especially important after the Reformation; every European state had religious minorities ("dissenters" from the state religion), and from now on the government could deal with them however it wished, without fear of interference from an outside power or church in sympathy with that minority.

The importance here should be clear: **national states**, as "states" (governments) became much more powerful and unified than before. Louis XIV could say without irony "I am the state" because he could expel the Protestant Huguenots from France and not worry about what Protestant England thought about it. This held sway for about a century and a half. Then events in America and France changed everything.

Revolutionary Nationalism

Both the American and French Revolutions shared a common philosophical foundation: the **Enlightenment** with its emphasis on human *reason* and the *universal* applicability of it to mankind's problems: all humans were basically the same, and endowed with the ability to think and reason towards "Progress." The Enlightenment thinkers had also seized on the idea of the "improvability" of mankind and human institutions.

Enlightenment "Civic" Nationalism

Two new elements in this **Nationalism** were *popular sovereignty* and Locke's concept of the *Natural Rights of Man*. *Popular sovereignty* literally means "rule of the people" and is the principle whereby government is based on authority granted to it by the population as a whole. Locke's *Natural Rights of*

Man was the basis for the related idea that government's primary purpose was to protect the individual and corporate rights of the populace. In one word, this is our modern concept of **Democracy.** Its practical expression (how it worked out in "real life") was—and is—that individuals in a "free" society are no longer "subjects" (bound to obedience) but *citizens* who give their assent (or consent) to the ideas and values of their society. This voluntary assent is what makes someone an "American" or a "Frenchman." Notice that you can hardly talk about **Democracy** this way without **Nationalism** showing up as well! (People love their country because they rule their country.)

These ideas were soon incorporated into founding documents in both America and France. For instance, the American *Declaration of Independence* (1776) famously proclaims:

> We hold these truths to be self-evident, that **all men are created equal**, and are endowed by their Creator with certain **inalienable rights**; and that among these rights are Life, Liberty, and the Pursuit of Happiness.
>
> From Merriam-Webster's Collegiate® Dictionary, 11th Edition ©2016 by Merriam-Webster, Inc. (www.Merriam-Webster.com)

Eleven years later, the writers of the U.S. Constitution made clear that the new government's authority would be derived from the consent of the governed in its opening phrase (rendered in "all caps" in the original): "WE THE PEOPLE of the United States . . ." They then attached ten "Amendments" (the "Bill of Rights") listing the freedoms that the government committed itself to protecting: freedom of speech, expression, religion; freedom from arbitrary search and seizure, from self-incrimination, and so on. This is still one of **Democracy**'s greatest achievements. In France, these ideas were expressed in the *Declaration of Rights of Man & Citizen* (1789): *"The source of all sovereignty resides essentially in the nation."* Or, instead of *"L'Etât, c'est moi,"* the French people declared, *"L'Etât, c'est nous."* (*"We* are the state.") This is the most succinct expression of **Democracy.**

From 1789 on, in many Western nations, formerly coerced subjects were converted into citizens voluntarily providing financial and military support in exchange for political freedom and economic stability (after the 1940s, this was called "social security"). **Nationalism** had truly met **Democracy.** They were and are mutually supporting ideals.

Romantic "Ethnic" Nationalism

For four days (October 16–19, 1813), one of the largest battles in European history raged: the Battle of Leipzig in Germany, also called the "Battle of the Nations," in which Napoleon's *Grande Armée* was decisively defeated by a coalition of "Allied" powers: Russia, Austria, Prussia, and a collection of militia volunteers from the various German states. As a result, Napoleon was driven out of "Germany" for the first time since his successful invasion in 1806. French **Nationalism** had been introduced to German-speaking people, but with an unexpected (for Napoleon, at least) result: many Germans had deeply resented French occupation of their lands, and eagerly joined the "War of Liberation" after Napoleon's disastrous Russian campaign of 1812.

As the fighting proceeded, German theorists began dreaming of a unified German state to replace the collection of kingdoms, princedoms, dukedoms, bishoprics, and republics that had constituted "Germany" for centuries. French and Enlightenment ideas were influential, but seemed "foreign," and were ultimately rejected in favor of more "modern" ideas. The Napoleonic era saw the birth in Europe of a "cultural revolution" that rejected the rational, universal values of the Enlightenment in favor of emotional, local loyalties and attachments. This movement, which deeply affected art, literature, and music, was called "Romanticism." It proclaimed the superiority of spirit and feeling over reason and logic; re-asserted religious values, calling for an intense individual "experience" of God; and gave credence to ancient folk tales about ghosts, elves, dark forest realms, and immortal heroes and warrior gods drawn from Norse and Germanic myth. Drawing from this deep, dark well of legend, folklore, and faith, German thinkers created a new, uniquely *ethnic* **Nationalism** that sought to create a community based on common ancestry, language, and culture. Rather than see mankind as a "family," these theorists saw a "jungle" of competing nationalities, each with "rights" of its own that must be preserved and asserted. Each nationality had been born with a unique *Geist* ("spirit"), derived from a long relationship with unique *Boden* ("soil"), which in turn formed a unique *Volk* ("people, folk"). Of course, Germans thought themselves the *most* unique. One did not "become" German by choice, inclination, or immigration (the way someone can "become" American); a true "German" was only *born* as such. In the middle of the 19th century, the Kingdom of Prussia, led by its dynamic prime minister, Bismarck, fought a series of wars that transformed the German states into a single state, the *Reich* ("Empire"). A century later, frustrated German pride at losing the First World War, combined with deeply established ideas of German ("Aryan") ethnic and racial superiority (threatened by mixture with racially "polluted" and "degenerate" peoples like Jews and Slavs) would be most forcefully expressed by Adolf Hitler. The result was a Second World War and the "Holocaust." Unfortunately, it is possible to have **Nationalism** *without* **Democracy;** the outcome is often disastrous. This is sometimes called "Fascism."

Napoleon, Apostle of Nationalism

Columbus was responsible for the **Columbian Exchange**; Martin Luther launched the Protestant Reformation and opened the door to the free-thinking age of the Enlightenment; John Locke laid out a rationale for a government responsive to the will of the people, **Democracy.** While it is difficult to argue that one man "invented" **Nationalism,** it is easier to see who did more to *spread* nationalist ideas than any other person: Napoleon Bonaparte.

Napoleon Bonaparte, 1769–1821

He is remembered (correctly) as one of the greatest military commanders of all time; as "Emperor of the French" he very nearly became "Emperor of the Europeans" as well. But his lasting historical importance goes far beyond the military academy textbooks:

- First, Napoleon spread the *Ideals* of the French Revolution across Europe and beyond (foremost among these: **Nationalism & Democracy**);
- Second, he dreamed and worked for a united Europe (bitterly opposed by Britain) that is still the basis for the European Union (which Britain has just voted to leave!)

- Third, Napoleon created a "Confederation of the Rhine" in Germany, reducing 300+ states to about 30; ironically, he helped inspire German unification!
- Fourth, he was an "apostle" (missionary) of **Nationalism** to many non-French peoples: Germans, Italians, Balkan peoples (Greeks, Serbs, Romanians), Arabs (he briefly invaded Egypt in 1798–99), even the Latin Americans who rebelled against Spain and Portugal in the 1820s;
- Fifth, even after his death (1821) he inspired various *revolutionary movements* in Poland, Russia, the Ottoman Empire, and the Austrian Empire in 1848 and after.
- Finally, he opened the door to generals seizing power over their countries: from Benito Juarez and Simon Bolivar in Latin America in the 1820s to Francisco Franco in Spain in the 1930s, to Muammar al-Qaddafi in Libya in the 1960s and Gamel Abdel Nasser and Abdel Fattah al-Sisi in Egypt (1950s and 2014), the principle of civilian control of the military has been upended in favor of military control of the government. Napoleon was not just a general, but a general who seized power.

All of these "achievements" of Napoleon have one thing in common: **Nationalism**: the aspiration (successful or not) to unite a people into a powerful *state* protecting and promoting the interests of their *nation* (however defined). It is the most powerful idea in the history of the world. It has built powerful nations (the U.S., Israel, Germany) and destroyed empires and multi-ethnic states (the Ottoman empire, the Austro-Hungarian Empire, Yugoslavia, the Soviet Union). It unites and divides. It is the "universal political solvent." It is the primary source of wars and upheavals in your world today. And when combined with **Democracy**, it can build a powerful, affluent and stable society.

THINKING IN TIME

1. Using Kohn's definition, would you call yourself a "nationalist"? Why/why not? If not, where is your "supreme secular loyalty"?

_____

_____

_____

_____

_____

_____

2. Think of ways that Nationalism & Democracy can be mutually reinforcing.

_____

_____

_____

_____

_____

_____

3. In what ways to do you think Nationalism could be compared to religion?

_____

_____

_____

_____

_____

_____

FOUNDATION 4

INDUSTRIALIZATION & CAPITALISM

The Columbian Exchange

Globalization and Acceleration

The Rise of the West

Industrialization and Capitalism

Nationalism and Democracy

About 1760 a wave of gadgets swept over England.[1]

—a schoolboy

*The wealth of those societies in which the capitalist
mode of production prevails, presents itself as
"an immense accumulation of commodities,"
its unit being a single commodity.*[2]

—Karl Marx

Historian Eric Hobsbawm referred to the transformation of world history
from 1789 to 1848 as the era of the "dual revolution": the French Revolution
and its major ideas, which we examined in the last section (**"Nationalism &
Democracy"**); and the Industrial Revolution which appeared in Britain at
about the same time.[3] I have borrowed his model to discuss the transformative changes that, over the last 240 years, have created the "modern" world
we live in. Before we dive in deeper, let's take a moment to review where we
have already been.

The Columbian Exchange of agricultural goods, Eurasian domesticated
animals, microbial organisms, and human populations transformed the
Atlantic into a Euro-African "lake" and made possible the rather sudden
expansion of European ("Western") political, economic, cultural, and military power into the Americas and eventually into Asia and Africa as well
(**"The Rise of the West"**). I call these developments the first and second
Foundations of the Modern World. The Columbian Exchange laid the
groundwork for **The Rise of the West,** which, in turn, expressed itself in
two ways: the first *political* and *ideological* (**"Nationalism & Democracy"**)
and the second *economic* and *social* (**"Industrialization & Capitalism"**).
It is to this second outgrowth of **The Rise of the West** that we now turn,

---

[1] Quoted in T.S. Ashton, *The Industrial Revolution* (Oxford: Opus/Oxford, 1997), 48.

[2] *Capital,* Vol. 1, in *The Marx-Engels Reader.* 2d ed. Ed. Robert C. Tucker (NY: W.W. Norton, 1978), 302–303.
A commodity is anything that can be bought or sold. Under capitalism, *anything* and *everything* is or can be a
"commodity."

[3] *The Age of Revolution 1789–1848* (NY: Barnes & Noble, 1962), ix.

but try to keep this in mind: the two trends were *simultaneous* and *mutually influential*! I often think of them like two wheels connected by an axle, like a "Segway," with the course of modern world history rolling forward relentlessly.

Ksenia Usata/Shutterstock.com

Production & Investment

Warning: this part of the Guide is going to read a bit like your "Economics 101" text book. But it is necessary. **Foundation 4** is really about two basic economic activities that people perform: *Production* (making things or harvesting crops that are necessary or desired) and *Investment* (putting wealth to work in order to yield more wealth). I am being deliberately vague because really *anything* can be "produced" or "invested." And note this: what is "produced" can be "invested," and *vice versa*. It may help if we break it down further.

Economists often refer to three "Elements of Production": land, labor, and capital.

Elements of Production

1: *Land*: to grow food, produce ore, provide space for a factory
2: *Labor*: people to work
3: *Capital*: can be
    a) *material* used in production (capital goods)
    b) *money* invested in production, to create profit (financial capital)

From Merriam-Webster's Collegiate® Dictionary, 11th Edition ©2016 by Merriam-Webster, Inc. (www.Merriam-Webster.com)

As the box points out, *land* is the most basic and original "element of production." We use it to grow our food as well as to mine ores and fossil fuels to produce energy and the metals we need. In the industrial era, it also serves a humble but necessary function: to provide a convenient place and space for a *factory*, a facility where desired products are made from raw materials by consuming energy. But land is just space without the second element of production, *labor.*

Land is potentially useful and productive, but without *labor* (people to work on it to raise crops or dig ore out of mines) it remains useless scrub or open pasture. *Labor* is also a form of **investment** itself;—you put something in and, hopefully, you get more out. But workers aren't free;—they *cost* money to hire (or purchase, in the case of slaves), which means *labor* requires an additional **investment,** of *capital*, the third element of production.

As you can see in the box, *Capital* comes in two forms, *material* and *monetary*. *Capital* is whatever is **invested** to produce something of increased value (in addition to the *labor* we mentioned above). Raw materials (coal to provide energy; iron to be converted to steel; even *land* to build factories on) are relatively low value substances that, when "worked" by an industrial process, yield a higher value product. Finally, *capital* is also the *money* (in whatever form; it can be "cash" or credit) that is **invested** to start and/or maintain a productive process (a mine, a factory, a retail business); it pays for *land*; it pays for *labor*; it pays for *capital goods* . . . if this seems confusing, it really isn't. The fact is that all of these "elements of production" can function as "*capital*" at any given time. Even *labor* can be a "capital good":—when you have a population rich in trained workers you haven't hired yet, that is like sitting on a gold mine or an oilfield.

Capitalism

"Capitalism" is one of those big words that is thrown around by many people who really do not know what it is. ("Socialism" is another.) One writer of a brief introduction simply declares that "capitalism involves the investment of money to make money."[4] He then goes on to say it's a bit

---

[4] James Fulcher, *Capitalism: A Very Short Introduction.* (Oxford, 2004), 18.

more complicated than that. There are several elements or components that make up **capitalism.**

Elements of Capitalism

- The employment of *capital* (wealth) to create more *capital* (profit)
- The creation and/or distribution of *capital* by means of *market forces* (such as the "law of supply and demand")
- Wealth/property can be held in private (individual/family) hands
- The use of *wage labor* to produce goods for a "free" market, with wages determined by *market forces* and paying for goods and services produced by capitalist businesses

From Merriam-Webster's Collegiate® Dictionary, 11th Edition ©2016 by Merriam-Webster, Inc. (www.Merriam-Webster.com)

In earlier times, the primary purpose of production (food, tools, building materials, etc.) was consumption. You produced what was needed and little else. When non-essential items were produced, they were usually "luxuries" intended for **trade.** (See Volume 1 of this *Student's Guide,* **Principle 4.**) Often this trade was more about diplomacy and dynastic interests than anything else. This slowly changed as local economies grew more diversified (producing a wider variety of things) and more efficient (capable of producing more of a thing); this created *surpluses* that were both a blessing and a curse: you could get more stuff if you had more stuff to trade with; but you had to find more people to trade with. With the evolution of **Capitalism**, this changes. By selling and trading skillfully, one could produce a profit (monetary/material *gain*); one could then use this gain to produce more profit through **investment** in new products, skills, or markets. This is why we say that a hallmark of **capitalism** is its drive to "reproduce" capital. You operate in such a way that you are constantly producing *more wealth.*

The way you operate is in a "free market." This is an environment in which the **capitalist** (one who deals with **capital**) is more or less "free" to buy and sell and "wheel and deal" with minimal interference from outside players (government; predators; religious rules and morals). A big part of this is the freedom to own *property* and to dispose of it (particularly to leave it to heirs), again with minimal interference from outside players (government; predators; religious rules and morals). In most modern states, property can be *taxed* (a portion of its value handed over to pay for government services) but cannot be *seized* without "due process of law." (You should recall that this was promoted by the Englishman John Locke, whom we met in **Foundation 2** above.)

Finally, **Capitalism** revolutionized *work*. In earlier times, just as food was grown and products made for consumption, so the people who grew food and made things were compensated with food, clothing, and anything else they needed (paid "in kind"). Money didn't enter into it because there was almost none. This began to change after 1500 with the discovery of massive silver mines in the Andes mountains of South America, which not only made metallic ("hard") money more available, but also encouraged the introduction of paper currency and credit systems based on the availability of silver. This in turn led to two more innovations:

1. *Food production* became *commercialized* (food was now produced to be sold in markets, in exchange for money; such produce—much of it not edible, like sugar, tobacco, and cotton—we call "cash crops"); farming thus became a business; **and**

2. Labor became *commercialized* (workers paid "in cash"). Just as **production** is now directed toward a market, so labor itself is subject to the market: from now on, in **capitalist** societies, the worker must "sell" his *labor* to the "highest bidder" he can find. But in reality, he is in competition with other workers needing jobs; so he just becomes the "lowest bidder," offering his labor for whatever the market is willing to pay him. And, of course, if workers are paid in cash, there must be products for them to buy, and workers, factories, and entire industries to produce for this expanded "consumer economy."

Industrialization

If you can imagine the modern world economy as a computer, then **Capitalism** would be the "software" and **Industrialization** would be the "hardware." Just as we saw that **Nationalism & Democracy** operate together, so the **Industrial Revolution** fueled *and was fueled by* **Capitalism,** and *vice versa.* They can exist and function apart, but it is only in combination that they transformed the modern world, and continue to contribute to the Fifth **Foundation, Globalization & Acceleration.**

The *major elements* of **Industrialization** are:

1: The transition from making things by *hand,* one at a time, to making them with *machines* in *mass* quantities;

2: The *Concentration of Labor:* the transition from individual artisans working in "cottage industries" to *masses of workers* producing goods in *factories.*

3: The transition in transportation from reliance on muscle power to *steam-driven* engines.

From Merriam-Webster's Collegiate® Dictionary, 11th Edition ©2016 by Merriam-Webster, Inc. (www.Merriam-Webster.com)

"Around 1780 came the Industrial Revolution in England. Incomes per capita began a sustained growth in a favored group of countries around 1820. In the last two hundred years in the most fortunate countries real incomes per capita rose 10-15 fold. The modern world was born. The Industrial Revolution thus represents the single great event of world economic history, the change between two fundamentally different economic systems."[5]

The **Industrial Revolution** was quite simply the most important, transformative "event" to take place in human history since the adoption of **Agriculture (Principle of Civilization 2).** Like that earlier "revolution", this one was a change in the method of *production.* **Agriculture** was the "mass production" of a *surplus* of food with *muscle power*; **Industrialization** is merely the "mass production" of a *surplus* of everything—(including food)—using *machine power.* This transition continues to change the entire world we live in (see **Foundation 5).**

---

[5] Gregory Clark, "The Industrial Revolution," Univ. of California-Davis Working Paper, 2013, p. 2. "Per capita"means average per person.

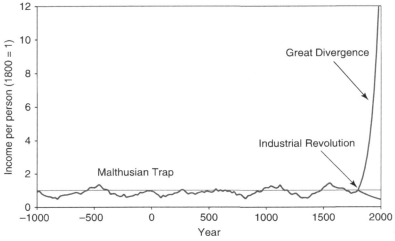

Assembling department, National Cash Register, Dayton, Ohio demonstrates mass production of precisely made complex products achieved during the 19th century.

British Birth

Historians have long noticed the striking fact that the changes we associate with the arrival of **Industrialization** first appeared in Great Britain. There are many reasons for this, but I will start with a factor I highlighted in the previous *Student's Guide:* **Geography is Destiny (Principle of Civilization 1)**. Britain is first of all a large island, facing the North Sea and Scandinavia to the east, the Channel and

France to the south, and Ireland and the North Atlantic to the west. Except for its Scottish and Welsh hinterlands, the island is dominated by the ancient land of England, mostly flat, with no major river systems, but many small streams and coastal inlets. As its population steadily grew in medieval times, its forests were nearly annihilated to provide wood for fuel and building material; its arable land intensively farmed to the point that its population soon outstripped its grain harvests. Nevertheless, England was blessed with abundant coal and iron deposits near the surface; and its topography made canals and railroads easy to build, with short distances to cross lacking the harsh environments found in Russia and America. Please go to the following link to see a map of Industry from 1715–1815: http://pammack.sites.clemson.edu/lec122sts/IRmap.gif

In addition to **Geography**, Britain had other advantages now seen as crucial to its success in transitioning from **Agriculture** to **Industrialization.** I call them the "Four Ms":

Why Britain Was First

- **Men** (labor surplus)
- **Materials** (raw materials: coal, iron, sheep's wool)
- **Markets** (colonies: sources of raw materials & customers for manufactures)
- **Money** (*capital* for investment: Bank of England)

From Merriam-Webster's Collegiate® Dictionary, 11th Edition ©2016 by Merriam-Webster, Inc. (www.Merriam-Webster.com)

Britain had a ready supply of *labor* due to both population increase (helped along by the effects of the **Columbian Exchange** and changes made in **Agriculture** that increased efficiency and output) and what has been called the "enclosure movement." This can be described as another aspect of the *commercialization* of **Agriculture**: many landowners in England, wishing to increase their incomes and improve their standard of living, began to notice the growth of the textile industry in the Netherlands and its ever-increasing demand for wool. These landowners realized that England's grassy landscape and temperate climate was perfect for breeding sheep, so they began to convert their grain-producing fields into sheep pastures. One "knock-on" effect of this was to throw thousands of farm laborers out of work (and literally "off the land") as they were no longer needed to tend sheep. A Tudor nobleman, Sir Thomas More, in his *Utopia* even described this as sheep eating men. In the short term, this process led to rural unemployment and crime; but this problem soon solved itself in the early 1800s as demand for factory labor skyrocketed.

Britain was similarly blessed with *raw materials* in the form of rich iron and coal deposits that were easily accessible. These two minerals are the twin keys to the early **Industrial Revolution,** because coal replaced wood and other "biomass" as dependable fuel sources. Coal (converted into "coke" by burning) sustains higher temperatures for longer periods, and more evenly. This made possible hotter furnaces to carbonize iron into *steel* that could be shaped to make both iron rails and the trains that could be carried on them. One can also speak of sheep's wool as a "raw material," because it was converted into wool thread and then cloth by mechanical spinners and looms that could be powered by *steam,* the major technological breakthrough that launched the **Industrial Revolution.**

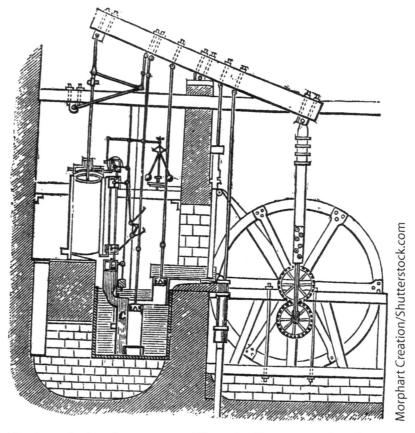

Morphart Creation/Shutterstock.com

Watt Steam Engine, vintage engraved illustration. Trousset encyclopedia (1886–1891).

The steam engine used coal to generate heat to boil water in a closed cylinder; the steam was then condensed in a different cylinder to create a vacuum. It was soon discovered that steam could *push* a piston, and the vacuum could *pull* it back. This meant that combining these two artificially contrived motions could turn a wheel, an axle, or drive a push-pull/rotary motion engine. Burn enough coal, boil enough water, and you can create a wagon that propels itself.

AVA Bitter/Shutterstock.com

So Britain had the *raw materials* at hand to advance into the industrial age. But even where it lacked, it could travel to other parts of the world to get what it needed.

Above we used the word *markets* to describe arenas where goods and services are bought and sold. Britain was blessed here too. Thanks to its island **Geography,** England evolved as a naval power soon after 1492 and began to expand overseas, first into neighboring Ireland and then into the North American continent, where it established its first permanent settlement at Jamestown, Virginia in 1607. New England developed as a haven for the religiously disaffected, but all of the colonies were financed in the beginning by businessmen and government interested in getting access to *raw materials* (foodstuffs, cash crops like tobacco, lumber) for transport and sale at home. But later, as the colonies grew, they became *markets* of a different sort: places full of people needing finished products ("manufactures") from the homeland (furniture, fine clothing, ships and sailcloth). It was the American colonists' dissatisfaction with being the colonial "periphery" to England's manufacturing "core" that helped inspire the Revolution, and the establishment of the United States as a manufacturing "core" in the 19th century. But **industrial** nations require both parts of this relationship to be successful: *materials* to make production possible, and *markets* to sell the products to. But there is a final piece to the puzzle of the **Industrial Revolution:** a different type of "fuel."

To capitalize on the possibilities of **Industrialization,** money was also needed, in the form of **capital.** We saw above that **capital** appears in two forms: material and monetary, and it is in the latter sense that we are examining it here. "It takes money to make money," and **Industrialization** is quite simply the most expensive human activity ever devised. Unlike **Agriculture,** which requires *land*, *labor*, and *capital* (material, in the form of seeds, animals, and tools) but not necessarily money, industry (whether a mine, a factory, or a railroad) requires money *capital* to purchase the *land*, hire the *labor* (wage workers), build the factory or mine or railroad, and finance the material *capital* in the form of machinery, machine tools, railway tracks, and so on. Britain's **capitalists** had acquired great wealth through the Caribbean sugar trade and were looking for ways to invest their *capital* to create more *capital*. A huge boon to this was the creation of the Bank of England in 1694. Originally chartered to act as a source of credit for the monarchy, it soon expanded into a "national bank" that could lend credit on the basis of anticipated tax and tariff revenue, charging interest on the amounts borrowed, and rewarding its depositors with part of that charged interest, keeping the difference as its own profit. England also boasted a number of private banking houses, the most famous being Lloyd's and Barclay's. With large amounts of cash and credit available, industrialists could borrow the vast sums needed to launch their industrial enterprises, paying the loans back from their profits and then reinvesting in their own or others' industries. The process began to feed on itself in a type of "feedback loop." In this way, **Industrialization** fed, and was fed by, **Capitalism.**

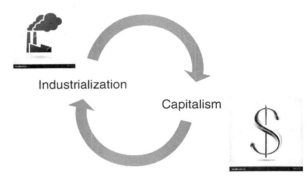

Industrialization

Capitalism

"Long Divisions": The Social & Cultural Effects

Just as the adoption of **Agriculture** led directly to all the forms of human inequality we find around us, so **Industrialization** only made that inequality more permanent and nearly inescapable. It has transformed every aspect of human life, and appears to be irreversible; we couldn't "go back" to the old way even if we wanted to. We call it the **Industrial *Revolution*** because the changes were accomplished so rapidly that many people had trouble adjusting to them; the times we live in are being rapidly revolutionized by computers, cell phones and the Internet. Just ask your grandparents (or parents!) how they lived before computers, and you'll realize how rapidly life has changed. The 19th century era was a similar period of wrenching change. Here are just some of the ways society was shattered by **Industrialization & Capitalism:**

• *Population Growth:* Again, just as **Agriculture** increased food production, allowing for expanding population growth, **Industrialization** had the same effect, only more so. Steam power, in particular, revolutionized food production by allowing human and animal labor to be replaced by machines (tractors, combine harvesters, etc.); railroads made possible the speedier transportation of foodstuffs from the farms to the cities, and steamships allowed transport of food across the oceans in shorter and shorter times. Vacuum-sealing and refrigeration only improved these trends. More fresh food available at ever-lower prices steadily increased and improved the diet (don't forget **Foundation 1!**) and raised birth rates, making even more workers available. In 1798, Thomas Malthus published an *Essay on Population* that argued that all human societies were trapped in an endless loop of overpopulation and starvation driven by the iron ratio of the physical limits of available farmland to the almost limitless human capacity to reproduce. **Industrialization** broke us out of the trap by raising the "ceiling" on how much food could be produced. The other side of the ratio, however, remains, and is posing a challenge to 21st century global society. "A tremendous change occurred with the industrial revolution: **whereas it had taken all of human history until around 1800 for world population to reach one billion,** the second billion was achieved in only

130 years (1930), the third billion in less than 30 years (1959), the fourth billion in 15 years (1974), and the fifth billion in only 13 years (1987)."[6]

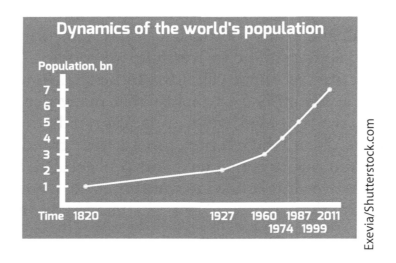

- *Class Conflict:* Just as **Agriculture** created two major social divisions (landowners and land-workers), so **Industrialization** fostered the appearance and growth of two new classes: the "*bourgeoisie*" (or "middle class") owners of the "means of production" (factories, mines, banks, businesses, and all the professions that serve these: lawyers, accountants, managers, etc.); and the "*proletariat*" ("working class"): those who perform various tasks in exchange for money wages. In the Middle Ages, the landowners and "peasant" workers at least benefitted from a mutual interest: everyone needed to eat, the landowners were fed by the peasants and the peasants received protection from the landowner. The **capitalist** system reduces every function to a relationship to *money*: thus the manager pays the worker to work, but he tries to pay as little as possible to extract as much work as possible; the worker's interest lies in working as little as possible for as much money as possible. Again, medieval landowners rarely tried to reduce their peasant workforce, since this would most likely reduce the size of the harvest; but factory managers maximize profits by keeping operating costs to a minimum, and no cost is higher (or easier to reduce) than labor/wage costs. They employ as few workers as possible to get the job done. Another way wages were kept down

---

[6] See text and graphs available at www.worldometers.info/world-population.

was by maintaining a "free" market in labor: by forcing workers to compete against each other for available jobs, they bid their own wages down to meet the employer's demands. This led workers to form *unions* to collectively bargain for wages and hours by eliminating/reducing this competition between workers.[7] The relative powerlessness of the worker at the hands of the business owner inspired the reform movement called "Socialism" and led Karl Marx to predict a massive uprising by workers against the **capitalist** system itself that would usher in a "new age" of production that would abolish money and all forms of private property in favor of a society that produced and distributed "from each according to his ability, to each according to his needs": "Communism."[8] Although to date there has not yet been a true "workers' revolution" against **capitalism,**[9] there is no doubt that the "class conflict" remains a reality for the vast majority of people around the world today.

Everett Historical/Shutterstock.com

Karl Marx (1818–1883)

---

[7] This is an instance of **Principle of Civilization 3** from the previous Student's Guide: **"Clashes of Culture Drive Innovation"**: in this case, the "owner culture" clashing with the "worker culture" to create both labor unions and business cartels.

[8] Phrase quoted from Karl Marx, "Critique of the Gotha Program," in *The Marx-Engels Reader,* 531.

[9] The "communist" revolutions in Russia, China, and Cuba did not "liberate" workers from oppression, but instead re-enslaved workers by replacing **capitalist** corporations with monolithic "party-state" dictatorships; not at all what Marx had in mind.

- *Materialism:* This could also be called "consumerism." **Industrialization** made available unprecedented amounts and varieties of every commodity imaginable (and quite a few that, until recently, were *un*imaginable). Not only were the material necessities of life (food, clothing, and shelter) more accessible, at lower process, than ever before in human history, but an array of products that often served no rational purpose were produced, advertised, and sold. About a century ago, specialized shops ("butcher, baker, candle-stick maker") began to give way to large interior "department stores" like Macy's in America and Selfridge's in Britain; by the middle of the last century, these in turn were increasingly replaced by or incorporated into massive suburban "shopping malls" that promised not only the wide variety of products and services increasingly affluent consumers demanded, but an entire shopping "experience." Consuming became a form of entertainment.

This also affected work. By the end of the 20th century, "production" jobs (where people were paid to make things for sale) were largely replaced by the kind of jobs you have probably already experienced: "service" jobs (where people are paid to meet the demands of others: cooking/serving food; waiting on customers; providing specialized customer/technical support, etc.) The author of this book has never worked in a factory, but he has at various times in his life sold encyclopedias door-to-door, worked in a shopping mall bookstore, cleaned a fast-food restaurant, and worked in telephone customer service for a bank. Both **Industrialization & Capitalism** made these jobs and millions of others like them possible and profitable.

- *Environmental Issues:* As you may recall from the *Five Principles of Civilization* (see pp. 20–21), the blessings of **Agriculture** came with a cost: Deforestation and Soil Erosion as well as "over-cropping "and "mono-cropping" (growing one plant or crop exclusively and repeatedly in the same spot because it is more efficient and profitable to do so). **Industrialization** only intensified humanity's use and abuse of the planet's ecosystem. Raw materials like wood, iron, and silver; "fossil fuels" like coal, oil, and natural gas; specialized and rare substances like uranium and bauxite (which is used to make aluminum) all have to come from the ground, above it or below it. The intensive "harvesting" of these substances cannot be done without damaging the plant, animal, and microbial life nearby. The burning of fossil fuels and other matter produces toxic chemical pollutants that are released into the atmosphere as well as into water sources. Finally, around World War II, artificial *plastics* were invented. These chemical compounds could be shaped into anything imaginable and mass-produced, especially into food and drink containers which were "disposed of" when no longer needed. But most of these plastics are not "bio-degradable," meaning that they do not break down easily, but remain in the environment for decades, often for centuries, further damaging the ecosystem we all depend on. We have just become aware of the problem in the past few decades: the coming century will determine if we can reach equitable global solutions to these problems **Industrialization & Capitalism** have created.

Huguette Roe/Shutterstock.com

- Finally, there is the **Acceleration** of everyday life. Your life and mine are simply much more busy and fast-paced than a few decades ago. **Industrialization & Capitalism** have made it possible to go farther, faster, to more places, to make more money, to spend more money, and to entertain ourselves, than any civilization in the history of the world. On average, we work fewer hours per day and per week than our parents and grandparents did, so we have more leisure time and more ways to fill it. But we need to spend money to entertain ourselves, and this requires good-paying jobs that are increasingly scarce thanks to the drive to automate (employ computers and robots to perform tasks humans and animals used to). Our lives are governed by increasingly accurate time pieces (watches, clocks, cell phones) that help us determine when are we are supposed to be where. Without this regimentation, life as we know it would fall apart. By the way: don't be late to class!

Conclusion

I have thrown a lot at you in the last few pages, but that is only because **Industrialization & Capitalism** have thrown all of humanity into both organization *and* disarray. We are both blessed and cursed by these momentous changes, and we are forced to cope with the consequences of these changes *as they are taking place,* and even as the changes seem to be changing! (Ask yourself: what model phone do you carry? Is there a new model coming out soon? What "apps" are available for it? How many new apps have you installed in the last month? How old is your computer's operating system? How is it different from the previous one? You get the idea.) There are just two closing thoughts I want to leave you with as I end this chapter:

1. *The "West" and the "Rest."* **Industrialization & Capitalism** are the prime factors in **The Rise of the West.** Because these changes began in (and for long decades remained exclusive to) the "Western" world (Europe and America), they were developed by the West and then "exported" (often by force) to the "Rest" of the world (Asia and Africa). Much of the history of the last two centuries is dominated by this one trend.

2. **Globalization & Acceleration**: The Fifth and last **Foundation of the Modern World** will be discussed in more detail in the next section of this *Student's Guide,* but I want to introduce it to you here. The changes brought about by the first four **Foundations of the Modern World** continue to expand in *time and space:* they have reached the entire globe and at an ever-increasing speed are transforming human life. This is where we are, and how we got here.

NAME _____

1. What's the difference between the two types of "capital"?

_____
_____
_____
_____
_____
_____
_____

2. What are some ways that **Capitalism** promoted **Industrialization**? And vice versa?

_____
_____
_____
_____
_____
_____
_____

3. Is there an alternative to **Capitalism**? Can you imagine a society not operating this way? What would it look like?

_____
_____
_____
_____
_____
_____

FOUNDATION 5

GLOBALIZATION & ACCELERATION

The Columbian
Exchange

Globalization and
Acceleration

The Rise of
the West

Industrialization and
Capitalism

Nationalism and
Democracy

Globalization is a fact of life.
But I believe we have underestimated its fragility.[1]

—Kofi Annan, UN Secretary General 1997–2006

If you're totally illiterate and living on one dollar a day,
the benefits of globalization never come to you.

—Jimmy Carter, US President 1977–1981

We started this journey through the history of the modern world by following Columbus's ships as they crossed the Atlantic. The Genoese navigator thought he was searching for a new sea trade route to East Asia (the "Indies"). As we saw, he didn't find what he was looking for, but he found a whole lot that he was *not* looking for: new plants, animals, minerals, and other resources (including land, land, *land*). In addition to everything else that comes to mind when we think of Columbus and how he unwittingly transformed the world, he can also be considered someone who opened a door to a new age of mankind: the age of **Globalization.** And another effect of this development was the **Acceleration** of human history and development. We will conclude this second volume of the *Student's Guide to World History* by exploring each of these in turn.

Globalization Defined

Peter N. Stearns writes in a useful overview that **Globalization** is "the process of transformation of local phenomena into global ones . . . a process by which the people of the world are unified into a single society and function together."[2] The term "globalization" is rather new, and when most people hear the word, they think of aspects of it that are rather new (the Internet, live global news/sports broadcasts, etc.), but is **Globalization** itself "new"?

Most historians would say no. In fact, one of the hallmarks of World History is the tendency of all of the various human communities (to varying degrees, to be sure) to reach out to and interact with other communities. This

---

[1] Address to World Economic Forum, Davos, Switzerland, Jan. 31, 1999. Found at http://www.un.org/press/en/1999/19990201.sgsm6881.html.

[2] *Globalization in World History.* (Routledge, 2009), 1. This is also the source of the Jimmy Carter quote that opens this chapter.

tendency began with the rise of civilization itself, as tiny agricultural communities in the Tigris/Euphrates, Nile, Indus, and Yellow river valleys coalesced into larger towns and cities; the cities then combined to form "states," and the states evolved into kingdoms and empires. What seemed to drive this community building was a twin desire: mutual protection and commerce/trade. As we saw in the previous volume of this *Student's Guide,* **Trade is the Lifeblood of Civilization,** but it must be said that, without security, trade is nearly impossible. So the desire to exchange goods went hand-in-hand with the need to feel "safe." And both are easier to achieve over wider, broader areas.

The "Great *Convergence*"

World History has evolved over time in what looks like a series of "ebbs" and "flows" as human global society ("Civilization") has expanded and contracted, as highly organized agriculture-based urban societies have trespassed onto nomadic migration routes, occasionally being driven back into their core areas in disorder. But overall, the trend has been in one clear direction: the organized societies ("civilizations") have gradually won, expanding onto new territories and holding them, corralling nomadic/traditional societies into "safe areas" or absorbing and assimilating these peoples into the civilized culture[3]. According to William H. McNeill, by the 300s BCE, as many as four major civilized "empires" expanded far enough to touch each other and begin to engage in limited long-distance trade[4]. Other historians point to later eras, particularly about 1000 CE, as the first of several "eras of globalization." (Others suggested are 1500, 1850, and our own era,—1945 to the present.[5]) Common to all of these eras are tendencies toward political and military expansion twinned with increased exploration and trade (and, as you learned in the first volume of this work, **trade** also fostered the flow of ideas and technologies across the world). This process could be called the "Great Convergence," and is one of the highly visible features of the colorful mosaic of World History.

For the purpose of this *Student's Guide,* I have chosen the approximate date of 1500 CE to denote the first "globalization era." As you saw in the first section

---

[3] See Vol. 1, *The 5 Principles of Civilization*, Principle 3: **Clashes of Culture Drive Innovation**.

[4] See *The Rise of the West: A History of the Human Community*, chapter VII, "The Closure of the Eurasian Ecumene."

[5] See Stearns, *Globalization in World History*, Chapters 3–5.

of this book (**The Columbian Exchange**), the discovery of the Americas and their integration into the "Western" political/economic network altered the trajectory of human history, shifting the "center of gravity" of civilization away from Asia toward Europe and, eventually, the Americas themselves. This shift I have labeled **The Rise of the West**, a phrase I borrowed from William H. McNeill's book of the same name. It is a major component of **Globalization**, because the "flavor" of the world's convergence has been almost exclusively "Western" (Euromerican): even the way events are dated is in accordance with a Christian calendar, rather than a Muslim, Jewish, or Confucian one.

As we saw in the second section of this guide, part of the reason for the West's "Rise" has been its almost unique tendency to look forward rather than backward, to welcome innovations and new technologies, to abandon or sideline traditional ways of thought if they were found no longer useful. Even the Christian religion conformed itself and re-molded its teachings under the continual influence of Greek rationalist thought; this tendency is visible up to and through the Protestant Reformation, which rejected authoritarian pronouncements by clergy in favor of reasoned interpretations of the received texts of the Bible, and eventually accepted the possibility that Christians could disagree "in good faith" about its teachings.

This religious and intellectual "non-conformity" opened the door to the twin political ideologies of the 19th century, **Nationalism & Democracy.** These concepts, in which political power was to be vested and nested in national states governed by popular consent, ran against the prevailing currents of traditional Eurasian governmental authority, which were characterized by vast multi-ethnic empires governed by hereditary monarchs. This "altered trajectory" of the West was both influenced by and fed the growth of a unique **Mentality** (see Vol. 1).

But perhaps the most visible, tangible transformation the world has seen dates from about 1850: **Industrialization & Capitalism,** as we noted in the previous section, turned people's lives upside down across the Western world, and very soon did the same to people across Asia and Africa. In about a century or so, the entire world was drawn into a web of interdependence based on an "internet" of steel rails, copper wire, and the wakes of steamships thrusting through the worldwide waves, annihilating space and time, reducing travel time from months and weeks to days and hours (eventually, with jet air travel, to hours and minutes), and diminishing the lag time of communications from days and hours to minutes and seconds. These changes originated in the European nations, but soon spread to the entire world, thanks to the success of the overseas empires (especially the British, French, and Dutch) in exploiting the technological and financial opportunities **Industrialization & Capitalism** made possible. The "Great Convergence" was complete by 1950, ruling a world in which a person could travel from any point on the globe to any other point on the globe in less than 48 hours, and could speak to any other person on the globe by telephone (soon augmented by satellite) instantaneously. One can sense the mood of optimism of the early post-war period by reading the Charter of the United Nations, and by recalling that the 1940s saw the rise of a vigorous "One World" movement.

Unfortunately, what **Globalization** gave with one hand, it could take away with the other.

The "Great *Divergence*"

I borrow this term from a book about Chinese economic development by Kenneth Pomeranz,[6] but I think it applicable on a global scale. For all the ways that **the Columbian Exchange, the Rise of the West, Nationalism & Democracy,** and **Industrialization & Capitalism** created a common human experience of the world, these very same developments and trends also created fissures in the human community that will continue to plague us into the foreseeable future.

While **the Columbian Exchange** created a culinary common market and increased the total food production of the world, it also spurred the enslavement of millions of Africans over four centuries, perhaps the darkest period of humanity's inhumanity. The Atlantic slave trade sought to justify itself by the fiction of African racial inferiority, a doctrine that played a role in bringing about the American Civil War of the 1860s, resisted the Civil Rights movement of the 1960s, and continues to affect the American political and social fabric as these words are being written. Of course, Africans were not the only people to be oppressed, enslaved, and in some cases annihilated by European bigotry. **The Rise of the West,** which introduced "enlightened" ideas about the "brotherhood of man" and his infinite capacity for self-improvement, paradoxically sought to spread these ideas through ruthless campaigns of conquest and imperialistic expansion. There is perhaps no better personification of this seeming contradiction than Thomas Jefferson, third President of

---

[6] *The Great Divergence: China, Europe, and the Making of the Modern World Economy* (Princeton, 2000).

the United States, who famously penned the most revolutionary and liberating sentence in history: "We hold these truths to be self-evident, that all men are created equal, and are endowed by their Creator with certain inalienable rights; and that among these rights are life, liberty, and the pursuit of happiness." Yet he owned hundreds of slaves, and negotiated the Louisiana Purchase, which not only doubled the land area of the fledgling United States, but also opened the door to a long twilight of aggression, exploitation, and expulsion of Native Americans by European-Americans. In this way, the process set into motion thousands of years earlier by the expansion of the first civilizations in Eurasia was completed in modern times on the opposite side of the planet. The "Divergence" between "civilized," "modern" societies and their "primitive" counterparts has only intensified, though efforts are now underway to preserve remnants of the natives' cultures and languages.

Jefferson is also a personification of the third **Foundation, Nationalism & Democracy.** Again, we are confronted by a paradox: the right of all peoples to self-government, in a state organized around a common identity of interests, would seem to have encouraged a different level of "brotherhood of man," in the form of a "family of nations." And this was the hope that fostered the birth of the unsuccessful "League of Nations," as well as the still surviving "United Nations Organization." But the experience of the past century also demonstrates that, rather than bringing the world's peoples together in peace and cooperation, **Nationalism & Democracy** have done the opposite: democratic politics have been misused to aggravate ethnic, racial, and religious tensions; and loyalty to one's own "nation" (or ethnicity) is easily perverted into hatred for another's, and a willingness to fight (and perhaps die) to destroy the other in order to preserve one's own. It must be said that at the heart of the United Nations itself lies a perhaps fatal flaw: in the name of human global unity and peace, it accepts and promotes the continued existence of separate, squabbling nation-states; dreaming of "One World," it dedicates itself to preserving the frontiers we have erected around ourselves. "Good fences make good neighbors." But all the neighbors are *not* "good": in fact, few are.[7]

---

[7] This "cross-current," "good news, bad news" take on the present condition of the world is informed by two bestselling books that appeared in the 1990s; the first, which saw the end of the Cold War as a new era of democratic globalization, was answered (rather crankily) by the second, which argued that the world was coming apart at the religious/cultural seams. Take your pick. See Francis Fukuyama, *The End of History and the Last Man* (Avon, 1992) and Samuel P. Huntington, *The Clash of Civilizations and the Remaking of World Order* (Touchstone, 1996).

The 20th century (1900s) could be called the "**Globalization** Century." It really began in 1914, when a "civil war of the West" broke out, a "second 30-Years War" fought (as was the previous one of the 1600s) around Germany. This time, between 1914 and 1945 Germany made two bids for world supremacy (with an "intermission" of 21 years), betting that its political model (Ethnic **Nationalism** without **Democracy**) combined with its economic might (**Industrialization &** state **Capitalism**) would bring victory. Instead it brought two massive defeats, disruption of **Trade** patterns around the world, scores of millions of deaths, a "Great Depression" in between the wars, a "Convergence" of the world in the common experience of war and liberation, and a "Divergence" as the industrialized world separated into mutually hostile capitalist and communist camps: the "Cold War."

Just as problematic as the national "divergence" developing along "horizontal," spatial lines, is another even more troubling "vertical" divergence. Just as **Nationalism & Democracy** drove human communities apart along ethnic and/or religious fissures, the rapid expansion of **Industrialization & Capitalism** has driven yet other fault lines between and across societies, this time those of wealth and class.

The Great Divergence: "Brandt Report," 1979

"North" (Modernized World)	"South" (Developing World, inc. China)
• 25% of world's population	• *3 billion people (75% of world's population)*
• 80% of its income	• *20% of world income*
• *average life expectancy >70 years*	• *Average life expectancy <50 years*
• *he or she will rarely be hungry, & will be educated at least up to secondary level*	• *poorest countries: one out of four children dies before age 5; one-fifth or more suffer from hunger and malnutrition; 50% have no chance to become literate*

Geography seems to play a role here. In 1979, Willy Brandt, former Chancellor of West Germany, chaired an independent commission on international development issues that produced a report bearing his name, the "Brandt Report." It showed that the world's richest and poorest, most- and least-developed nations grouped themselves respectively north and south of a line drawn on a world map. Thus, at a time when "East" and "West" were beginning to lose their meanings (the "Cold War" between the Western democracies and the USSR would not survive the decade), it became clear that a new, even more troublesome global divide had appeared, between "North" and "South." **Capitalism** was the major driver of this development; multinational corporations like Microsoft, GE, and Exxon/Mobil, each richer than many entire countries, could almost ignore national boundaries. Meanwhile more wealth was created than ever before in human history.

Global Output

1900	$2 trillion (thousand billion)
1950	$5 trillion
2000	$39 trillion*

*(1995–98 output exceeded previous 10,000 years combined!)

But clearly, this wealth is very unevenly distributed.

The "Great Divergence": The Income Canyon

- 71% (5.3 billion people) either "poor" (income <$2/day; 1.1 billion) or "low income" ($3–9/day; 4.2 billion)

- 13% (790 million people) "middle class" (income $10–20/day)

The forces of **Globalization** are driving the massive changes sweeping the world. Great leaps forward in computer and satellite technology are drawing human beings closer together than ever before. However, as we have seen, the changes have created massive disparities in wealth and economic activity. *Population Growth* is yet another complicating factor; as the previous section of this guide indicated, the world's population is (at this writing) 7.5 billion and rising steadily. It is not just food production that is under stress; thanks to **Industrialization & Capitalism,** humanity continues to burn increasing quantities of fossil fuels to maintain the standard of living of the affluent societies. Not only does this endanger the environment, but it raises a

"Malthusian" question: how much of these non-renewable resources are left? Could we run out? When? And if so, then what?

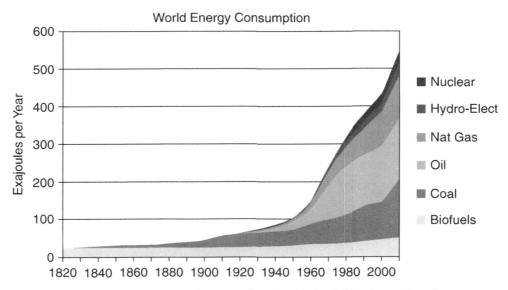

Figure 1. World Energy Consumption by source, based on Vaclav Smil estimates from Energy Transitions: History, Requirements and Prospects together with BP Statistical Data for 1965 and subsequent years.
Found at https://ourfiniteworld.com/2012/03/12/world-energy-consumption-since-1820-in-charts/

As you can see, it is not clear how much longer this can go on. The **Acceleration** of all of these trends is easily seen. One last table will illustrate the increasing pace of human development:

The "Stone Age" lasted over 1 million years . . . then
- Agriculture began   10,000 YA ("years ago")
- Complex societies (Civilizations) arose   5000 YA
- Industrialization began   200 YA
- Technological society appeared   50 YA
  (electronics, computers, satellites, Internet)

Globalization & Acceleration are *bringing us together* and *driving us apart* at the same time. We who are living in the 21st century are the beneficiaries and the victims of over 7,000 years of human social, political, and economic change and development. Humanity clearly has the intelligence and drive to improve its material existence (as least for some); it also has the technical means of self-annihilation through both nuclear war and self-inflicted eco-logical collapse. You are a part of that story, and a key to its outcome.

History, in brief, is an analysis of the past in order that we may understand the present and guide our conduct into the future.

—Sidney E. Mead

THINKING IN TIME

1. Peter Stearns says that **Globalization** is "the process of transformation of local phenomena into global ones . . . a process by which the people of the world are unified into a single society and function together." Is this a complete definition? Describe what you think **Globalization** means.

_____

_____

_____

_____

_____

_____

2. List some ways that you have experienced the **Acceleration** of changes in your own life and of those around you.

_____

_____

_____

_____

_____

_____

3. In your opinion, have you and your family been helped or hurt by **Globalization**? Employ specific examples to support your argument.

_____

_____

_____

_____

_____

_____

ANNOTATED BIBLIOGRAPHY

Those of you who are interested in "the Big Picture" might want to explore these works that examine humanity's story from the widest possible perspective—including theories as to how and why humanity's civilizations have developed as they have. It includes military, economic, social, cultural, scientific, geographical, and environmental approaches. Whatever your interest, you should find something on this list.

Appleby, Joyce. *The Relentless Revolution: A History of Capitalism.*

Archer, Christian et al. *World History of Warfare*
An example of the "new military history": how and why we fight.

Aries, Philippe and Georges Duby, eds. *A History of Private Life* (5 vols. in total)
Vol. 4 *From the Fires of Revolution to the Great War*
Vol. 5 *Riddles of Identity in Modern Times*
Fascinating overview of changing mores, family customs, and values, and how these changes have produced modern society.

Armstrong, Karen. *A History of God*
The Battle for God
Fields of Blood
The world's foremost author on religious faith and its history.

Boorstin, Daniel. *The Creators*
The Discoverers
The Seekers
Group biographies of the most influential human beings in history: artists, explorers and thinkers/spiritual leaders.

Braudel, Fernand. *A History of Civilizations*
  The Mediterranean & the Mediterranean World in the Age of Philip II (2 vols.)
  Memory & the Mediterranean
  Civilization & Capitalism
      Vol. 1 *The Structures of Everyday Life*
      Vol. 2 *The Wheels of Commerce*
      Vol. 3 *The Perspective of the World*
  A French historian who "made history" as a World War II POW, a founder of the "*Annales* school" that refocused attention on economic and social factors in history and interpreting change as an evolutionary process (*la longue durée*).

Burbank, Jane and Frederick Cooper. *Empires in World History: Power and the Politics of Difference*
  Winner of the World History Association Book Prize, a massive overview of mankind's largest, most enduring institution.

Burke, James. *The Day the Universe Changed*
  Turning points in human understanding, focusing on scientific and technological "leaps forward" that continue to shape our modern world.

Burke, James and Robert Ornstein. *The Axemaker's Gift: A Double-Edged History of Human Culture*
  The role of axe makers ("rocket scientists") in human history.

Cameron, Rondo. *A Concise Economic History of the World*

Cannadine, David. *The Undivided Past: Humanity Beyond Our Differences*

Cartwright, Frederick. *Disease and History.*

Christian, David. *Maps of Time: An Introduction to Big History*
  And he means BIG—man's place in the Universe!

Crosby, Alfred. *Ecological Imperialism*
  The Columbian Exchange (both accounts of species transplanted to Americas)

The Measure of Reality (how Western Civilization quantified everything)
Throwing Fire (a history of gunpowder and projectile weaponry)
Children of the Sun (a history of energy consumption/exploitation).

Curtin, Philip. *Cross-Cultural Trade in World History.*

Diamond, Jared. *Guns, Germs and Steel: The Fates of Human Societies*
   Collapse: How Societies Choose to Fail or Succeed
      Very influential best-sellers—and controversial. A biologist attempts
      to explain the origins of human inequality.

Ferguson, Niall. *The Ascent of Money*
   Empire
   The War of the World
   Civilizations: The West and the Rest, others.
   Histories emphasizing the role of money and finance

Fernandes-Armesto, Felipe. *Millennium: A History of the Last Thousand
   Years*
   Civilizations: Culture, Ambition, and the Transformation of Nature
   The Americas: A Hemispheric History, others
      Very readable, combining climatic and cultural approaches.

Frieden, Jeffrey *Global Capitalism: Its Fall and Rise in the Twentieth
   Century*

Fukuyama, Francis. *The Origins of Political Order*
   From Political Order to Political Decay

Fulcher, James. *Capitalism: A Very Short Introduction.*
   Haywood, John. The Great Migrations
   Human population movements and their effects.

Hobsbawm, Eric. *Nations and Nationalism Since 1780: Programme, Myth,
   Reality*
   His classic study of Nationalism and its legacy.
   The Age of Revolution 1789–1848
   The Age of Capital 1848–1875

The Age of Empire 1875–1914
The Age of Extremes 1914–1991

Jay, Peter. *The Wealth of Man*
A history of money, its forms and uses.

Jones, E.L. *The European Miracle: Environments, Economies, and Geopolitics in the History of Europe and Asia*
An argument for the role of geography in explaining the "Rise of the West."

Keegan, John. *A History of Warfare*
A classic overview by the foremost military historian of our time; a social and cultural approach to how, where, and why men fight.

Kennedy, Paul. *The Rise and Fall of the Great Powers*
Another classic study; this one of how nations become "Great Powers," and how they lose that status: "imperial overstretch."

Landes, David. *The Wealth and Poverty of Nations*
Like Diamond, an attempt to employ geography to explain economic and wealth disparity across the world.
The Unbound Prometheus is a classic study of technological change since 1750.

Mann, Charles C. *1491: New Revelations of the Americas Before Columbus*
1493: Uncovering the New World Columbus Created
More on the "Columbian Exchange."

Marks, Robert. *The Origins of the Modern World: A Global and Ecological Narrative from the Fifteenth to the Twenty-First Century.*
A useful overview.

McNeill, William H. *The Rise of the West: A History of the Human Community*
Plagues and Peoples
The Pursuit of Power
A World History

Keeping Together in Time: Dance and Drill in Human History
The Human Web (with J. R. McNeill)
The author most influential on my approach. The "dean" of World History.

Morgan, Curtis F. *The 5 Principles of Civilization: A Student's Guide to World History, Vol. 1.*
The previous volume in this series. The foundations of the "Foundations."

Morris, Ian. *Why the West Rules—For Now*
An examination of the "Rise of the West."

Piketty, Thomas *Capitalism in the Twenty-First Century*
A recent bestseller and controversial classic.

Ponting, Clive. *A New Green History of the World*
The global environment and human history.

Roberts, J. M. *History of the World*
Illustrated or not, one of the most readable surveys available.

Sass, Stephen L. *The Substance of Civilization: A Material History of the World*
A study of the "stuff" that civilization is made of.

Standage, Tom. *A History of the World in 6 Glasses*
An Edible History of Humanity
Food & drink in human history.

Stearns, Peter N. *Globalization in World History*
The Industrial Revolution in World History
Readable and informative overviews.

Thomas, Hugh. *World History*
A readable overview.

Turchin, Peter. *War & Peace & War: The Life Cycles of Imperial Nations*
A discussion of imperialism.

Wallerstein, Immanuel. *The Modern World System* (4 vols.)
Historical Capitalism

Well-written examinations of the role of capitalism in the modern world

Wolf, Eric. *Europe and the People Without History*
A classic examination of the "losers" in the "Rise of the West."